Malachi

Other Founders Study Guide Commentaries

- *1 Corinthians: Founders Study Guide Commentary*
  – Curtis Vaughan & Thomas D. Lea
  expositional comments on the book of 1 Corinthians

- *James: Founders Study Guide Commentary* – Curtis Vaughan
  expositional comments on the book of James

- *Ephesians: Founders Study Guide Commentary* – Curtis Vaughan
  expositional comments on the book of Ephesians

- *Galatians: Founders Study Guide Commentary* – Curtis Vaughan
  expositional comments on the book of Galatians

- *Acts: Founders Study Guide Commentary* – Curtis Vaughan
  expositional comments on the book of Acts

- *1,2,3 John: Founders Study Guide Commentary* – Curtis Vaughan
  expositional comments on the books of 1 John, 2 John and 3 John

Other Founders Press Titles

- *By His Grace and For His Glory* – Tom Nettles
  a historical, theological and practical study of the doctrines of grace in Baptist
  life: revised and expanded 20th anniversary edition

- *The Baptism of Disciples Alone* – Fred Malone
  sets out to prove that the Bible authorizes only credobaptism, the baptism
  of disciples alone

- *Dear Timothy* – Edited by Tom Ascol
  collection of writings from seasoned pastors contains over 480 years of
  combined ministry experience for old and new pastors alike

- *Ministry By His Grace and For His Glory*
  — Edited by Tom Ascol and Nathan Finn
  Essays in Honor of Thomas J. Nettles

- *Truth & Grace Memory Books (#1, #2, & #3)* — Edited by Tom Ascol
  a solid plan for children's Bible study, Scripture memory,
  catechetical instruction and exposure to great hymns

FOUNDERS STUDY GUIDE COMMENTARY

Malachi

Baruch Maoz

Founders Press

Committed to historic Baptist principles
Cape Coral, Florida

Published by

Founders Press

Committed to historic Baptist principles

P.O. Box 150931 • Cape Coral, FL 33915
Phone (239) 772–1400 • Fax: (239) 772–1140
Electronic Mail: founders@founders.org or
Website: http://www.founders.org

©2011, 2016 Baruch Maoz

Printed in the United States of America

ISBN: 978–1–943539–00–0

Dedication

This book is dedicated to my beloved grandchildren
Noam, Maya, Nadav, Yotam, Yonatan,
Caitlyn, Elinor, Yotam, Avishai and Eliya

in the hope and the prayer that they will come
to know, love, and serve Malachi's God,
who is none other than the God and Father
of our people's Messiah, Jesus of Nazareth.

I wish the same to each of my readers.

May we all love and serve Him
with the kind of faithfulness Malachi sought to promote.

Contents

Publisher's Preface

As a Jewish Reformed Baptist Baruch Maoz pastored the Grace and Truth Congregation in Israel from 1976 until his retirement in 2008. Since that time he has devoted himself to itinerant preaching, teaching and writing. This devotional commentary on Malachi is the fruit of his long, faithful ministry.

Founders Press is pleased to include *Malachi: A Prophet in Times of Despair* in our Founders Study Guide Commentary series. The Prophet Malachi ministered to a chastened but unrepentant people. As the last book in the Old Testament, this prophecy communicates God's judgment against His own people due to their spiritual formality and apathy. The message is as relevant today as when it was first proclaimed. Baruch Maoz has served the church of Jesus Christ well by explaining and applying this message in warm, practical ways that are faithful to text and to the larger context of the whole Bible.

Author's Preface

Malachi's prophecies suffer from unjustified neglect. His message touches an important aspect of life by teaching the essence of God's demands of mankind: Will God be satisfied with faithful ritual, or are His demands more fundamental, more heart-involving? If they are, how are we to identify them?

Malachi has wonderful things to say about marriage—a highly relevant message for today when marriage is so often challenged and its legitimacy undermined by selfishness. Another issue with which the prophet deals is disappointment, a common human ailment. The problems Malachi was sent to address were products of the way those who returned from Babylon handled their circumstances in contrast with the hopes they entertained.

This study of the prophet's message was originally written in Hebrew. In an effort to converse with English readers, I've modified the material while translating it. I assume English readers' concerns, interests, and assumptions differ slightly from those of an Israeli reader. Malachi's message remains unchanged, but its application differs with each audience. Rather than use a standard translation of the biblical text, I have provided my own. My purpose is not to offer a literary rendering but rather to draw your attention to the finer points of the prophet's language in a way that a normal translation would not. In the study of Malachi, it is important to be able to distinguish between cases in which the sacred name of God is used and those in which the prophet uses the Hebrew term *Adon* (אדון), meaning Master or Lord. I have therefore used LORD to indicate where Malachi uses the sacred name and *Lord* for those few cases in which he used *Adon*. This, I hope, will assist English readers to distinguish between the two.

As in all my devotional commentaries, my main goal is to clarify the text in a way that will encourage you to study and understand the Bible for yourself. But I may not and do not wish to handle God's Word in a merely technical manner. The principles enunciated by the prophets are meant to be guiding principles for our lives. I consider it my duty not only to point to the objective and universal meaning of the message, but to indicate some of its practical implications. You, dear reader, will decide if I have succeeded.

I have included a few quotes from Hebrew sources. Since this is a devotional commentary, I expect most of my readers will not have access to material in Hebrew. I have, therefore, limited the information on those sources to the name of the author. Any reader who may be interested in further research (and I hope my books will contribute to such an interest) will have no difficulty in finding the relevant sources.

The prayers at the end of each chapter are based on those of John Calvin in his exposition of Malachi. I consider Calvin to be the greatest of Bible expositors. He was a brave, God-fearing man, and a wise cultivator of his fellow men. He had a sense of the text, respect for its historical context, and an awareness of the relationship between one portion of Scripture with another. He directed his impressive abilities, his education, and his life experience toward the goal to which each of us should aspire: the glory of God. That is the essence of Malachi's message. It is the essence of the Christian life, and the goal of all creation.

I have been gratified with the warmth in which my commentary on Jonah was received and pray that this short work will likewise be useful to God's people.

Introduction

TO THE BOOK OF MALACHI

Malachi is the last of the Old Testament prophetic books. In Hebrew, it is made up of three chapters: fourteen verses in Chapter One, seventeen in Chapter Two and twenty-four in Chapter Three. In this book, we use the English division.

The Prophet

Nothing is known of Malachi's family or tribal background. The name Malachi appears nowhere else in the Bible. Some believe that it is not a name but an indication of the unknown prophet's calling to be a messenger of God (In Hebrew, Malachi (מלאכי) means "my messenger" (See Malachi 3:1). The ancient Greek translation of the Old Testament, known as the Septuagint, assumes such is the case, as does an ancient translation of the text into Aramaic (known as Targum Yonatan). Other ancient translations do not. The Talmud, an ancient Jewish interpretation of the Law and a repository of ancient legends, includes the view of one rabbi, who believed that Malachi was a pseudonym for Ezra the Scribe (Megilla 15a).

It is most likely that Malachi was the name of the prophet whose message is preserved in the book called by that name. Most prophetic books in the Bible introduce the name of the prophet, as Malachi is introduced, at the start of the book called by his name. If the reference of 1:1 was to a title rather than to a name, one would expect the text to say "the word of the LORD by the hand of *His* messenger" (malacho) rather than "the word of the LORD by the hand of *My* messenger."

Jewish tradition describes Malachi as "The Seal of the Prophets," and the Talmud (in Baba Batra 15:71) states that he belonged to the men of the Great Synagogue, an institution formed during the Babylonian exile that is said to have led the nation and played a large role in the formation of its early traditions. The history of this body is largely lost in the mists of time. Some doubt its existence. The Babylonian Talmud (there are two Talmuds: one written in Babylon and the other in Jerusalem. The former is considered more normative) in Megilla 17:72, states that the

Great Synagogue had 120 members, all chosen from among "the sages of Israel." But Megilla 81:5, 7 counts eighty-five members in all. The Jerusalem Talmud, in Berachot 82:5, 5, states that of the 120 members, 80 were "prophets."

The Great Synagogue, which most likely did in fact exist, does not seem to have had formal authority. Its authority was moral. It may have first been convened by Ezra the Scribe to serve as an advisory body with the intention of providing the people with spiritual and moral leadership.

One Jewish tradition states that Haggai, Zechariah, and Malachi all belonged to the Great Synagogue. Another tradition claims that Mordechai, Esther's uncle, was also a member. The reliability of such traditions is doubtful, if not downright impossible.

The Great Synagogue may have been the beginning of what later became the Sanhedrin. The Sanhedrin had seventy members, in accordance with number of Elders that advised Moses in the wilderness (Numbers 11:16). The Mishnah, a repository of Jewish tradition that precedes the Talmud and serves as its basis, states that the men of the Great Synagogue determined the Jewish canon (list of authoritative holy books), and that they formed the historical link between Moses and the Mishnah. By so doing, the Mishnah attributes to itself an authority equal to that of the Law, claiming to be the Oral Law handed down from Moses through the Great Synagogue and put into writing following the destruction of the temple.

The Historical Background

Why is it important to know the historical background of biblical books? There are a number of reasons.

First, the historical reality into which the Scriptures speak anchors their message in human realities. God's Word is not a mystical message from heaven, void of reference to human experience. Obedience to God does not allow us to cut ourselves off from the world God made and intends to redeem. The day will come when this world will visibly match God's will. That is why our Lord commanded us to pray for God's will to be done "on earth as it is in heaven" (Matthew 6:10).

In other words, the Christian faith is robustly earthy. While not addicted to this world, it has a great deal to do with it. Salvation is not being taken out of the world but being cleansed from the evil in it—and then going out to conquer the world for God. Christian obedience means involvement in every aspect of human endeavor with a view to the faithful implementation of God's will on earth and in anticipation of the day when that will be the case. The hope of the Christian message has to do with the redemption of the world and its reconstitution into the arena for the display of God's glory.

Second, an acquaintance with the historical background of the biblical message will help us understand the terms used and therefore the message. That message came from God. However, the need for it, its language, its content, the shape it took, and the terms it employed are all products of historical situations addressed by each passage. As we progress in our study of the book of Malachi, we will discover how an awareness of the circumstances into which Malachi spoke will greatly aid us in understanding the message.

The Bible was not written in mystical or angelic language but in human languages—Hebrew, Aramaic, and Greek. The message of the Bible is framed according to the rules of grammar, syntax, and human literary endeavor. The Holy Spirit guided men of God to write what He wanted them to write. But He did not obliterate the different personalities of the authors. That is why there are stylistic differences between Isaiah and Ezekiel, between John, Paul, and Peter. Both the historical context and the personality of the writer influence—sometimes determine—the meaning of phrases.

Third, familiarity with the historical circumstances to which the Scriptures refer enables us to connect between what was written and our own circumstances. This transforms study of the Bible into more than an intellectual exercise. This familiarity also enables the ancient message to become a message for us—and that is the primary value of Bible study.

In spite of the distance of years and cultures, human realities then and now do not essentially differ. The differences that do exist are superficial. God has not changed. He is today what He was yesterday and will be forever. Man remains man, and sin remains sin. He is still characterized by selfishness, laziness, pride, and an inordinate love of pleasure. He still prefers immediate, short-term advantages over long-term faithfulness to God. Man still struggles with disappointment and loss of vision. For those reasons, God's message through Malachi twenty-five hundred years ago is as relevant today as it was then.

The Jewish Community in Babylon

To obtain a good background for the message of Malachi, it would be useful to read the books of Daniel, Esther, Ezra, Nehemiah, Haggai, and Zechariah. They can all be read in just over two hours and make for a good read. Not too much effort is involved, but the value is great.

The Jews in Babylon settled and formed a large, increasingly wealthy, and influential community, with its own institutions. Some, like Daniel, Mordechai, and Nehemiah, held prominent posts in government.

The destruction of the temple and the repeated exile of aristocrats, professionals, and then the people of Judah, and the humiliation of the Judean king by proud, successful Babylon and its confident culture significantly impacted the exiles. There was a strong tendency to assimilate, or at least to adopt aspects of Babylonian culture. Evidence of this may be found in the Babylonian names adopted by prominent Jews: Sheshbazar, for example, was Zerubbabel's Babylonian name (Ezra 5:14; Haggai 1:4, 14; 2:2, 21). Mordechai (Ezra 1:2 and the book of Esther) was named after the Babylonian god Marduch. History knows of a Babylonian king with a similar name, Merodach-Baladan (2 Kings 20:12; Isaiah 39:1). In the Hebrew Bible, the list of returnees includes many whose names end with the letter א, a Babylonian spelling. Most of what are today assumed to be Hebrew names for the months of the year are, in fact, Babylonian. Since the calendar became extremely important to the Jewish people in Babylon (only by a careful maintenance of the calendar could they know when to celebrate the biblical feasts), the adoption of Babylonian names for the months testifies to the substantial impact Babylon had on the exiles, their culture, and their religion. Much of Ezekiel and Zechariah's amazing imagery is a reflection of Babylonian religious and royal imagery. Impressive examples of this have been found by archeologists.

In response to assimilatory tendencies, Jewish leadership increased its emphasis on the importance of the Law, the status of the temple, and the role of the priests as means of preserving national identity. True, there was no temple, but there was an avid hope for one, and a longing for the one that had been destroyed. To this very day, Jews mourn the destruction of the temple at the hand of the Babylonians. It was in Babylon that the expression, "The Law of Moses," became common Jewish idiom, viewed as summarizing the covenantal relationship between God and Israel.

The Jews in Babylon had no king, and the governor of Judea was a Persian appointee. This lent further importance to the priests, who assumed the national role they had in the days of the judges before Israel crowned its first king. A survey of references to the Law, the covenant, and the priests in the books of Ezra, Nehemiah, Haggai, and Zechariah will indicate the importance of these in the life of the nation. The priests were, of course, from the tribe of Levi and are therefore sometimes described in these books either as "Levites" or as "the sons of Levi." Thus, the temple, the Law, and the priests became the foci of national unity while the grounds for what later became pharisaical and later rabbinical Judaism were laid.

The Return to Zion

The circumstances surrounding Malachi's prophecies have to do with the return of part of the Jewish population from exile in Babylon according to the word of the LORD through Jeremiah (Jeremiah 25:11–12; 29: 10) and Daniel's prayer (Daniel 9:2). That return consisted of a number of waves and never included the majority of the exiles; the majority preferred to remain in Babylon.

Babylon was conquered in 539 BC by the united kingdom of Medians and Persians led by Cyrus. The first wave of returnees to Jerusalem was ordered by Cyrus (Ezra 1:1–11) in 538 BC, the first year of his reign. Isaiah had foreseen this long before it occurred (Isaiah 44:28; 45:1–7). Cyrus had no intention to reestablish the kingdom of Judea or accord the returnees political independence. He appointed a governor to run the civil administration and a high priest to serve alongside him (Ezra 3:2) and to lead the people in their religious affairs. He also decreed the reconstruction of the temple but not of the walls of the city. Cyrus was interested in the return of Judeans to the land because he wanted to bolster the Persian administration there and create an effective barrier between his kingdom and Egypt. Jewish resettlement could also serve to restrain the expansionist efforts of the Nabataeans.

Four years later, in 535 BC, after all due preparations, the first returnees left Babylon led by Zerubbabel the son of Shealtiel (Ezra 2:2, 68) and arrived in Jerusalem. Ezra 1–6 describes this first effort to settle the land. It is likely that Haggai and Zechariah were among those who arrived in Jerusalem at this time. After two years, in 534 BC, the returnees undertook the reconstruction of the temple (Ezra 3:8) with great excitement. They had no political aspirations and focused on reconstructing the temple (Ezra 1:5; chapters 3–4). Haggai and Zechariah, two prophets who were active at the time, dealt primarily with the temple and matters relating to the temple service (see also Ezra chapter 5).

The Samaritans, that hodge-podge of peoples brought into the land by the king of Assyria when he exiled the ten tribes and scattered them throughout his empire (721 BC, 2 Kings 17), hoped to join the returnees and become one nation with them (Ezra 4:1–2). Naturally, they did not like the idea of a reconstituted Judah in which they had no share because they (rightly) assumed such an entity would compete with them over hegemony in the land. They were rejected (Ezra 4:3) and, in response, adopted the policy of, "if you can't join them, beat them."

The Samaritans appealed to King Artaxerxes (Ezra 4:12–13), calling for a halt to the reconstruction. They insisted that Jerusalem was a notoriously rebellious city, and that restoring the temple would foment further rebellion. The Persians were always disturbed by such accusations because they faced repeated rebellions in their far-flung empire. The king therefore ordered a halt to construction, which continued until the second year of Darius the First's reign (522–486 BC, Ezra 4:24; chapter 5) in 521 BC—some thirteen long years.

There is some difficulty here, because Artaxerxes the First reigned between 464 and 424, years after the temple had been dedicated. He is an unlikely candidate for stalling its construction. The Persian king most suited to be the recipient of the Samaritan appeal is Cambyses, who reigned between 529 and 522. The book of Ezra names Artaxerxes as the recipient of the appeal, so we assume that Cambyses was also known in his day as Artaxerxes.

The returnees settled in a small enclave surrounding Jerusalem and engaged in restoring their religious, social, and economic life. The difficulties were real; construction was accompanied by strenuous Samaritan opposition (Nehemiah 2:10–19; 3:33–38; chapters 4, 6) even after Darius authorized it. The avid support of Haggai and Zechariah during what appear to be the final years of construction (520–516 BC) was very necessary. So, when circumstances dampened the people's spirits, Zechariah promised in the name of the Lord:

> This is what the LORD says: "I will return to Jerusalem with mercy, and there My house will be rebuilt. And the measuring line will be stretched out over Jerusalem," declares the LORD Almighty. Pro-

claim further: "This is what the LORD Almighty says: 'My towns will again overflow with prosperity, and the LORD will again comfort Zion and choose Jerusalem' " (Zechariah 1:16–17).

"Shout and be glad, Daughter Zion. For I am coming, and I will live among you," declares the Lord. "Many nations will be joined with the LORD in that Day and will become My people. I will live among you and you will know that the LORD Almighty has sent Me to you. The LORD will inherit Judah as His portion in the holy land and will again choose Jerusalem (Zechariah 2:10–12).

This is what the LORD Almighty says: "I am very jealous for Zion; I am burning with jealousy for her." This is what the LORD says: "I will return to Zion and dwell in Jerusalem. Then Jerusalem will be called the Faithful City, and the mountain of the LORD Almighty will be called the Holy Mountain."

This is what the LORD Almighty says: "Once again men and women of ripe old age will sit in the streets of Jerusalem, each of them with cane in hand because of their age. The city streets will be filled with boys and girls playing there." This is what the LORD Almighty says: "It may seem marvelous to the remnant of this people at that time, but will it seem marvelous to Me?" declares the LORD Almighty.

This is what the LORD Almighty says: "I will save My people from the countries of the east and the west. I will bring them back to live in Jerusalem; they will be My people, and I will be faithful and righteous to them as their God" (Zechariah 8:2–8).

In that connection, Haggai and Zechariah also spoke of great things concerning Zerubbabel, the son of Shealtiel (Haggai 2:20–23; Zechariah 4:6–7), leader of the returnees, and a scion of the Davidic line. Similar things were said by Zechariah about Joshua, the son of Jehozadak, the high priest who served alongside Zerubbabel (Zechariah 3:1–10; 6:9–15). Suddenly, Zerubbabel disappears from the pages of history. Perhaps the king got wind of what was said about him and ordered his return to Persia, where he died. We don't really know. Joshua the high priest continued for a time to play a role in the lives of the returnees.

Darius not only permitted the reconstruction of the temple, he provided generously for it. In 516 BC, the temple was dedicated amid much rejoicing (Ezra 6:15–22). But disappointment soon set in. The temple was an unsubstantial structure. The two prophets were commissioned by the LORD to encourage the people with a promise of the future (Haggai 2:1–9; Zechariah 4:8–10; 6:9–13; chapter 8; 14:7–21): The glory of this present house will be greater than the glory of the former house, says the LORD Almighty. And in this place I will grant peace, declares the LORD Almighty (Haggai 2:9).

This second wave was led by Ezra (Ezra 7–9) in the year 458 BC, during the reign of Artaxerxes the First, known as Artaxerxes Longimanus (464–424), arriving in the land during the seventh year of his reign (Ezra 7:7). It did not alleviate the situation, and Ezra, faithful to his priestly task (Ezra 10:15), called the people back to their spiritual heritage. On one occasion, he tore his clothes in public as a sign of mourning and cried out to God. His action finally gave rise to a sense of shame among the leaders, who undertook to mend their ways and rid themselves of their non-Israelite wives (Ezra 9–10).

Still, the state of affairs was grim. The temple was soon put to uses other than religious, and non-Jews were accorded access in direct contravention of the Law; the city was neglected; the Edomites and Samaritans controlled important agricultural and commercial areas; the number of returnees remained puny, even after some twenty thousand new arrivals joined the first returnees and settled in and around Jerusalem. Hopes were faint. There was an understandable tendency to turn from Israel's national aspirations and assimilate with other inhabitants of the land (Ezra 9:1–2). Even many priests followed such a course (Ezra 10:18).

The third wave was led by Nehemiah some thirteen years later in 445 BC, the twentieth year of Artaxerxes's reign (Nehemiah 2:1). Nehemiah was appointed governor of Judea and sought to encourage the people. He remained in Jerusalem about twelve years, working alongside Ezra in calling the people back to God's covenant (Nehemiah 8–10). The two initiated a renewal of the Feast of Tabernacles celebration, which Zechariah viewed both as important and portentous of the future (Zechariah 14:16–21).

Nehemiah was the first among the Jews to speak openly about repairing the walls of the city (Nehemiah 1:3; 2:10–18). Apparently, most of the returnees preferred to reside outside, in proximity to their fields and flocks. The economy was largely agricultural. There was little industry, very little administration, and no standing army. One of Nehemiah's main concerns was the fortification of Jerusalem, to which end he encouraged a Jewish population to take up residence within the walls (Nehemiah 7:4). He could do this because he enjoyed the trust of the king and would therefore not be suspected of provoking a rebellion. On the contrary, he represented the king in the land by serving faithfully as his governor. Nehemiah was also forced to take action against leaders among the people, who took advantage of the circumstances to enrich themselves by oppressing others (Nehemiah 4).

After governing for twelve years (Nehemiah 5:4), around 433 BC, Nehemiah returned to Susa (Nehemiah 13:6), where he remained briefly, returning to Jerusalem somewhere around 424 BC. In the course of his second visit, Nehemiah dealt with two problems that occupied Malachi a short while later: intermarriage between the returnees and women from the surrounding peoples and the neglect of worship in the temple (Nehemiah 13).

Malachi's Time

There is no direct indication of the time when Malachi was active or when the book of his prophecies was composed. The fact that sacrifices are offered and the temple *storehouse* was by then a familiar institution (Malachi 3:10; Nehemiah 10:38–39; 13:5) assumes a functioning temple. Since the temple was dedicated in 516 BC, it is fair to conclude that Malachi followed Haggai and Zechariah.

The priesthood in Malachi's day had been corrupted. This also indicates that he probably prophesied some years after the excitement that accompanied the dedication of the temple had dissipated. It is possible that he was active some time near Nehemiah's second visit to Jerusalem in 433. Some believe he was active in the course of that visit and in support of Nehemiah's reforms. Both men are concerned with intermarriage (Malachi 2:11; Nehemiah 13:23–27; see also Ezra chapters 9–10), both rebuke the people for neglecting to bring the tithe (Malachi 3:8–10; Nehemiah 13:10–14), and both speak of the oppression and materialism that had spread (Malachi 3:5; Nehemiah 5:1–13).

While all that is true, identity of issues does not necessarily imply identity of periods. Similar problems can arise at different times. The fact that Nehemiah mentions Haggai and Zechariah (Nehemiah 5:1; 6:14) but not Malachi seems to intimate that Malachi arrived on the scene later. If so, Malachi would have been active sometime after 424 BC and no later than 410 BC, because he speaks of Edom as an existing kingdom, and Edom was destroyed by the Nabataeans in 410 BC. We can therefore safely set the boundaries of Malachi's prophetic ministry as somewhere between 424 and 410 BC.

A Persian governor, titled Pasha (Malachi 1:8 in Hebrew), ruled in Jerusalem and tribute was paid to him. The title is actually Assyrian. It was adopted by the Babylonians and later by the Persians. Nehemiah was probably not the Pasha at this time because, during his tenure, he had forgone the right to receive tribute for governing. Instead, he supplied his household out of his own resources (Nehemiah 5:1). There is no reason to think that he would have acted otherwise had he governed during his second visit as well.

The Mood in Malachi's Time

A large part of the difficulty faced by the returnees of Malachi's time had to do with the dashing of their national hopes. They would have naturally assumed that the departure from Babylon, the renewal of national life in the motherland, the reconstruction of the temple, recommencement of God's worship, and the repair of the city's wall would lead to a national revival that would cause many of the Jews in Babylon to return as well. This, in turn, would be expected to spark the victory of Israel's faith in the world. Such expectations were cultivated by Israel's faith through the centuries. It is also what Haggai and Zechariah seem to have promised.

None of this happened. Instead, most of the people remained in Babylon. The few who returned were crowded into a tiny enclave while most of the country remained in the hands of foreign peoples. The Edomites had populated the south. The Samaritans ruled in Samaria. Galilee was inhabited by the Phoenicians, Aramaeans, and others. The restored temple was miniscule in comparison with the people's expectations, and the land suffered from drought and a locust invasion (Malachi 3:10–12). The Phoenicians established a colony in Jerusalem (Nehemiah 13:16) and commerce was conducted there on the Sabbath (Nehemiah 13:15–19). The Persian Empire, on the other hand, was at the height of its ascent. Its rule stretched from the Indus Valley in the east to the borders of Egypt and Ethiopia in the southwest and to the far northwest of what is now Turkey.

Instead of hearing the first peals of redemption and witnessing the extension of Israel's faith among the nations, the Jewish enclave was an insignificant pin's head. Confidence in Israel's calling and the desire to maintain a national identity had been greatly weakened in Babylon. They were further eroded by realities in the land. Many of the nation's leaders married non-Jewish wives (to do so, they apparently divorced their Jewish wives, which is why Malachi had to address the issue of divorce). Rather than the gentile nations embracing the faith of Israel, Jews were losing their national identity. Meanwhile, the nations of the region added to the economic difficulties imposed by the formerly neglected land, the unforgiving weather, drought, and locusts. An unfriendly local government, Nehemiah's absence, the lack of alternative national leadership and the weakening of the Davidic line imposed a heavy burden and oppressed the spirit of the people.

These circumstances would naturally impact the enthusiasm that originally brought the returnees to the land. People resorted to their own selfish interests, worship was conducted halfheartedly, and the sacrifices brought were the poorest of the flock and of the herd. Lack of enthusiasm led to despair. There seemed to be little reason to maintain a distinct national identity. This, in turn, led to an erosion of spiritual and moral loyalties, which is at the core of the subjects addressed by Malachi.

Subjects, Structure, and Literary Characteristics

Malachi's message is directed at the people as a whole (Malachi 1:1), but the primary focus is on the priests, the sons of Levi, appointed over the worship of God in the temple and over teaching the people God's ways (Malachi 2:1, 7, 13; 3:3). Those ways were to be understood in terms of the laws of the covenant God made with Israel at Mount Sinai. Malachi sought to show the people that the lack of blessing that they experienced was the product of their sins and those of their spiritual leadership. The Law said as much (Leviticus 26 and Deuteronomy 26–28).

Some among the people were bent on self-enrichment at the expense of social and national responsibility. It is likely that these are the *arrogant* (the Hebrew implies a body of individuals whose wickedness is calculated) and the *evildoers* of whom Malachi speaks in 3:15. Contrary to the Law, they oppressed the poor, satiated themselves with pleasure at the expense of familial stability, and indulged in witchcraft (2:14; 3:5). Most of these were priests, which in fact subjected them to Malachi's harsh rebuke (2:1–10) and made them liable to a future purge at the hands of God (3:5).

On the other hand, there were among the people those who feared God and supported each other (Malachi 3:16). Malachi's words were meant to encourage these faithful few. True, the state of the small remnant of God's people in Judea was nothing to be desired. But God is not subject to circumstances; He shapes them. He is sure to bring the day of redemption. Malachi sought to teach the people that God rules in spite of appearances.

The prophet called Israel back to God's ways. He called them to keep covenant by adhering faithfully to the Law. But the faithfulness to which he called was moral, not ritual, even when ritual issues were at stake. Sacrifices were to be truly sacrificial—they were to cost the people dearly because they were to be brought from the best of the herd and the flock, as the Law demands. God was to be honored by the people's devotion. If the priests would not honor Him by teaching and exemplifying these principles, they would bear the punishments which the Law prescribed. It was up to them to fulfill their priestly duties, guide the people in the ways of the Law, and obey the Law in the conduct of their daily lives and ministry without compromise and without reservation.

When Israel entered the land, God had forbidden the people to wed Amorites. In the same way and for the same reasons, women from the surrounding peoples were not to be taken as wives in Malachi's day. Covenant faithfulness involves sacrifice and self-control. He who is to come as herald of the day of redemption is described as *"the angel of the covenant"* (Malachi 3:1), an indication that the purpose of his coming is to fulfill the law of the covenant.

In the spirit of the prophets, Malachi's primary call is to obedience in terms of the Law. Israel should remain true and fulfill the requirements of the Law. They should not engage in witchcraft, adultery, or false oaths, nor should they hold back laborers' wages. They should care for widows, orphans, and foreign residents and pay the tithe. Only then can they expect the blessings promised by the Law, and only then will the nations be blessed through them.

Malachi's message ends with a call to remember the law of Moses, and a promise that God will send Elijah to save the country from the curse which the Law imposes on the unfaithful. Malachi speaks of the coming of the LORD in terms that do not take into account the nations of the world (3:1–5), although he earlier included them in God's kingdom and described them as subject to divine action (1:3–1, 11). His message is directed to Israel. Yet, Malachi accords God the title by which the kings of Persia described themselves and lords of all the earth: *The Great King* (1:14). It is in connection with such lordship that Malachi makes special reference to the Edomites as objects of God's sovereign action (1:2–5).

Like Jeremiah, Malachi bases his message primarily on the book of Deuteronomy, from which most of his quotations are taken and on which many of his statements seem to be based. Meaningful references (not quotes) also send us back to various parts of Genesis, Joshua, Isaiah, and Psalms. Obedience is all the more necessary in light of the approaching day of the Lord.

The language is largely prose. Some consider it quite pedestrian or void of literary style. From time to time, a rhythm may be detected by the Hebrew reader. There is a good deal of alliteration, detectable to those who read the prophet in the original language. The main literary features Malachi uses are those of contrasts and of dialogue: statements and resultant questions or responses. In many cases, the questions are, in fact, affirmations. Paul used a similar literary device in his letter to the Romans.

Malachi uses short, staccato sentences that lend sharpness to his words. Although his message comprises a short book, fifty-five verses in all, there are many alternative readings, the product of extensive copying (an indication of the book's importance). None of the alternative readings is of significance. Most seem to be a copyist's efforts to clarify what he considered obscure and therefore unlikely to belong to the original text.

Unlike most of the prophets, Malachi generally addressed his intended audience directly as if God Himself was speaking, without the instrumentality of a prophet. Only in 2:10–17 and 3:1–4 does Malachi quote. It is consistent with this feature that nothing is said, or even hinted, concerning the prophet, his background, or his history.

Malachi's Hebrew is unpolished. Some conclude that this is evidence that the prophet's words are given in their original from, without shaping them to literary conventions. Nevertheless, the book does have literary characteristics, all of which were common in ancient times. Here are a few examples:

1. Four-part dialogue: an opening statement or question, a response, a reply, and a rebuke or a promise.

2. Repetitious use of words of inquiry and reference: *where, but, if not, is it, why, in what, and what, for what, who, behold, I am/will.*

3. Contrasts: *I have loved Jacob, but Esau I have hated; They may build, but I will demolish; I the LORD do not change ... you, the descendants of Jacob, are not destroyed.*

4. Chiastic sentences (where the beginning and the end parallel each other): *loved Jacob ... Esau I have hated; parents to their children ... children to their parents.* The process of translation has obliterated the chiastic character of many sentences.

5. Alliteration, which is impossible to demonstrate in a translation.

6. Repetition: *loved you ... loved us; rebuild ... build; If I am ... If I am; If you do not ... if you do not; curse ... curse... cursed; reverence ... he revered; you have been unfaithful ... do not be unfaithful; return ... I will return.*

7. Couplets: *a son* and *a slave, a father* and *a master, lame* and *diseased, incense* and *pure offerings, send a curse* and *curse, life* and *peace, peace* and *uprightness, a root* and *a branch.*

It is surprising, but Malachi's language is almost pure Hebrew. There is no indication of Aramaean or Babylonian influence, such as may be found in Ezekiel, Daniel, and Zechariah, for example. Only one word (Pasha—in 1:8) is clearly not Hebrew. Another (רֻשַּׁ֫נוּ *we have been crushed*—1:4) may not be, although some relate it to the Hebrew word for poor (Jeremiah 5:17). The purity of the language is surprising because Malachi was born in Babylon, while Ezekiel and Daniel were born in Judea (we don't know much about Zechariah), and the language the latter two employ was obviously impacted by their environment. It is plausible that, contrary to views held by many in his generation, national identity was important to Malachi or to his parents, leading to a conscious effort to maintain purity of language.

Having said as much, we have noted a Persian kingly title attributed to God by Malachi (*Great King*, 1:14). He further adds that God's name is *Dreadful among the Nations* (another Assyrian and Babylonian title). Like the New Testament, Malachi thinks of Jehovah as the God of all nations as well as Him who established a covenantal relationship with Israel. The one concept does not contradict the other.

Although Malachi knows God to be dreadful, he does not consider Him so far removed from human realities that He cannot be addressed nor sympathetically understand those who address Him; He loves (1:2; 2:11), hates (1:3; 2:13, 16), is angry (1:4), tired (2:17), may be pleased and displeased (1:10, 13; 3:4), threatens (2:3; 3:11), blesses (3:10–12), and curses (2:2, 3, 9; 3:9).[1]

An important feature in the book of Malachi is the brief reference made to the Edomites (compare, for example, Ezekiel 36:35). The statement is most likely an intimation of the state of affairs that pertained to when the returnees arrived in the land and found large tracts of the south inhabited by the Edomites. This gave rise to a renewal of historic animosity between the two nations.

We should mention in closing that Malachi is the only prophet who accords Elijah, or a prophet who will function in the spirit of Elijah, the role of a herald prior to the coming of the Lord's messenger, the angel of the covenant. Jewish and Christian interpreters agree that the messenger is none other but the promised Messiah. Such a herald is without mention anywhere else in the Old Testament. The New Testament points to John the Baptist as the one who fulfilled this prophecy.

The book of Malachi may be divided into a prologue, seven sections, and an epilogue:

1:1 Prologue

1:2–5 Edom

1:6–14 Israel's Unworthy Sacrifices

2:1–9 The Priests' Unfaithfulness

2:10–17 God's View of Marriage

3:1–5 The Day Will Come When God Will Purge the People

3:6–12 The Tithe

3:13–4:3 The Day of the Lord

4:4–6 Epilogue: Elijah's role

---

[1] See Pieter A. Verhoef, *The Books of Haggai and Malachi, The New International Commentary on the Old Testament* (Grand Rapids, MI: Eerdmans, 1987).

Malachi and Other Old Testament Texts

The main connection between Malachi and other portions of the Old Testament is one of content and viewpoint, not of direct quotation or the use of motifs taken from other portions. Covenant and Law are important terms in Malachi's prophecies.

By way of example, Malachi refers to the books of the Law when he speaks of God's love for Israel (1:2) and of His discriminatory treatment of Jacob and Esau (1:3); when he describes God's fatherly relationship to Israel (1:6; 3:17), criticizes the people for dishonoring God's name (1:12), or speaks of the status of the levitical priests (2:1, 4–6) and of their special role (2:6–7); when he refers to the unity of the nation, issuing out a single parentage (2:10); to the unity of Adam and Eve, created "one" by God (2:15), and to the duty to tithe (3:8); when he describes natural disaster, such as drought and locusts, as the product of covenantal disobedience (3:10) as well as a curse on the land (3:17); when he speaks of the nations recognizing Jehovah's blessing on Israel (3:12) and of Israel's special position as a *treasured possession* (3:17—a highly uncommon term); of the law of Moses; and the title *servant of the Lord* that was accorded Moses and refers to the giving of the Law at Horeb (4:4).

Malachi also refers to other portions of the Old Testament when he speaks of Elijah the prophet (4:5), chastises the people for focusing on ritual rather than morality (2:13), describes God as both appellant and witness (2:14; 3:5), speaks of the day of the LORD (3:2, 19), of the purging of the servants of the LORD in the day of the LORD (3:3), of the people's former sins (3:6), and of the days when the nation was faithful and therefore pleasing to the LORD (3:4).

In addition, Malachi uses many terms that are either identical or similar to those used in other parts of the Old Testament. For example, *burden* (1:1), *from the rising of the sun to its setting* (1:11), *I will send the curse upon you* (2:2), *departed from the way* (2:8), *keep my ways* (2:9), *cut off* (2:12), *the widow, the orphan and the stranger* (3:5), *windows of heaven* (3:19), *drop their fruit* (3:11), *treasured possession* (3:17), *a root or a branch, ashes under the soles of your feet* (4:3), *Moses my servant* (4:4), *decrees and laws* (4:5), and *total destruction* (4:6).

In his extensive reliance on the Law, Malachi emphasizes the moral aspects of the Law, not the ritual. In this, he parts company with Haggai and Zechariah but follows the example of previous prophets, viewing the law of the covenant as a unity while making a distinction between its moral aspects and the civil and ceremonial. According to Malachi, the essence of obedience is not to be found in craven ceremonial adherence but in dedicated morality. He rebukes the people for a feigned obedience that does not involve the heart. He rejects religious practice that is strict about the letter of the Law while belittling it for lack of moral heart-involvement.

The title, *LORD of Hosts*, appears in this short book twenty-four times, making it the Lord's major designation in the book of Malachi. The proper name, *Jehovah*,[2] appears twenty-one times.

Malachi and the New Testament

Malachi is quoted or alluded to in the New Testament at least fourteen times, a surprising number in light of the size of the book:

Malachi	The New Testament
1:2–3	Romans 9:13
1:7, 12	1 Corinthians 10:12
2:10	1 Corinthians 8:6
3:1	Matthew 11:10; Mark 1:2; Luke 7:27
3:2	Revelation 6:17
3:5	James 5:4
3:6	Hebrews 13:8
3:7	James 4:8
4:2	Luke 1:78
4:5	Matthew 11:14; 14:12; Mark 9:13
4:5–6	Matthew 3:13; 17:10–11; Luke 1:17; John 1:21

[2] We need not enter here into a discussion of the proper way to pronounce the name. There is little importance to the pronunciation, so long as we are fully aware of the divine person being addressed.

CHAPTER 1

I Loved You
(MALACHI 1:1–5)

The burden of the word of the LORD toward Israel by the hand of Malachi: "I loved you," said the Lord, and you said, "How did You love us?" "Was Esau not a brother to Jacob"' says the Lord, "yet I loved Jacob and I hated Esau, and I made his mountains a desolation and his inheritance the dwelling place of desert foxes." Should Edom say, "We have been impoverished, but we will rebuild the ruins," this is what The LORD of Hosts has said: "They will build—and I will destroy. And they will be called 'the land of wickedness' and 'the people with whom God is angry forever' and your eyes will see this, and you will say, 'May the LORD be exalted beyond the borders of Israel.'"

As we turn to study Malachi's message, we should remember the importance of historical context. In the course of our study, we will try to penetrate the mists of time and understand the prophet's message in the context of the circumstances to which God sent His messenger.

This chapter presents us with God's message to the people as a whole. The next chapters have special reference to the priests. It is only fair to say that Malachi's message in chapter one would not have been necessary had the priests fulfilled their duties.

God's Love for Israel

The burden of the word of LORD toward Israel by the hand of Malachi. As is true of many of Israel's and Judah's prophets, Malachi's prophecies are described as a *burden*. Calvin reminds us that wherever this term appears in relation to a prophetic message, the message is one of stringent warning of approaching punishment. That is why, he further reminds us, the inhabitants of Jerusalem reacted as they did to Jeremiah's message when he spoke of the burden of the LORD (Jeremiah 23:38). They did not want to hear of such burdens and forbade the prophet to use the term.

This was no enjoyable message. It was not given to comfort the people or reassure them of God's goodwill. It was a message of sharp rebuke that demanded and was worthy of careful attention because it expressed the will of God for the people. We are not at liberty to speak as we wish to the people of our day. Like Malachi, it is our duty to tell them the truth about God and about themselves. Although not always a welcome message, it is needed nonetheless.

Though the term *burden* used by Malachi is identical to that used by other prophets, there is a difference. Most of the prophets spoke of *the burden of the Lord*. Malachi speaks of the burden of God's Word. He and Zechariah (Zechariah 9:1; 12:1) are the only prophets to use this phrase.

This *burden* did not come to the people directly. It did not drop down from heaven. It was not delivered by a divine voice or through an angel. It came through the instrumentality of an individual. God uses means. While He speaks to all, He does not speak to the majority, except through a prophet. Not all are teachers nor are all prophets, but all must hear and heed the message. God's Word is no less His Word today because it is heard through a preacher, who himself accesses it through Malachi and David, Moses and Peter, Paul and Jude.

Malachi did not commission himself. He was not his own messenger. God sent him. Malachi's message was not the product of his spirituality, wisdom, or intelligence, nor was it of his love of God and his justified concern for the people. We can safely assume that Malachi was characterized by each of these qualities. But his words were nothing less than the very words of God, spoken by inspiration of the Spirit of God. They are the burden of the word of the LORD by the hand of Malachi. The LORD commanded him to speak and told him what to speak. Malachi merely obeyed as should every minister of God's Word.

The burden of the word of the Lord is the message Malachi was sent to announce to Israel. In this case, Israel is but the remnant, a small section of the nation comprised of the relatively faithful who returned to the land rather than remain in exile in Babylon. The remnant is now addressed as Israel.

Malachi's message has ramifications that are wider than the fate of the returnees or even the nation of Israel as a whole. The message should be heard and heeded by those who returned and by those who did not, by Israel and by those who are not of Israel. It is to be heard and applied. Every application that can be drawn from Malachi's words for others is exactly that: an application, not the meaning of the words themselves. We need to learn to distinguish between understanding the message and applying it. The message was directed to a specific target audience. In this case, it was directed to the returnees from Babylon. After the message is understood, principles are to be derived. These then can be applied to any human group. To access the applications, we must first discover the meaning. We shall seek to do both in this book.

"I loved you," said the Lord. The people had sinned, but God opens His words of rebuke with a declaration of His love. That is what God is like. That is what His kind, gentle heart is like. He speaks of His love to sinners.

"I loved you." God was not saying, "I loved you in the past, but love you no longer." He spoke of His love in the past to show the force of His love in the present. God chose to relate to Israel in a discriminatory way, differing from the way He related to other nations. He loved Israel, and He proved His love in the course of history. Unlike many declarations of undying love people give one another, only to be forgotten in moments of difficulty or weakness, God's love has stood the test of time.

True love is unconditional. Malachi spoke of the love of God because he wanted to draw the people's attention to God's love for them in their contemporary situation. He loved them then, and He loves them now, in spite of their sin. The covenant of love which God made with Israel is as valid as is His undying love. True, Israel proved itself unworthy, but God's love is never earned. It is stubborn, undeserved, irrevocable. It does not depend on anything but His unchanging nature. Nothing, but nothing, can separate those whom God loves from the love He has for them.

In light of God's complaints against Israel, of which we will learn as we study Malachi, this declaration is as encouraging as it is surprising. The returnees were unfaithful. They made light of the worship of God and therefore of God Himself. Still, God declares, I loved you! Here is a picture of God's amazing grace, a grace that is not the product of what man does but of God's heart, His kindness, and His generosity.

How Did You Love Us?

"I loved you," said the Lord, and you said, "How did You love us?" Driven by the circumstances in contrast with the hopes they entertained, the returnees doubted God's love for them. That was the root of their sin. They were convinced that they deserved more from God. Not receiving what they expected, they responded like a spoiled child who accuses his father, like a selfish woman trying to force her will on her husband, "You don't love me anymore," "if you loved me, you would satisfy my demands." In light of their difficult circumstances, how could it be said that God loved them?

Of course, the answer was ready: the difficult circumstances in which the people found themselves were the inevitable, just result of their sin. That idea never entered their minds. So far as they were concerned, God should have been satisfied with the kind of worship they offered and, in response, was duty bound to bless them. Their selfish arrogance dimmed their sense of the awesome holiness of God and therefore their sense of sin, responsibility, and guilt. Unwilling to admit guilt and own up to responsibility, they preferred to accuse God. Mankind today behaves in a similar fashion by pointing at all the terrible things man has done to himself and insisting that, "If God exists, these events would have never taken place."

The returnees were ungrateful. They measured the love of God by what they received at that moment, forgetting the wonders of what they had received in past generations, even what they had received in their own time. God had created the nation, brought them out of Egypt, gave them His Law, and defended them from enemies. When they sinned, He rebuked them, warned them, and finally punished them, but always brought them back to Himself and restored His blessings. Their very presence in the land was evidence of His faithful love.

They had been cast out of the land because of their sins, yet brought back. For their sakes, God had brought down the mighty kingdom of Babylon and placed Cyrus on the throne, as Isaiah prophesied (Isaiah 44:28; 45:7–11). When they returned to the land and found a hostile people living there, He defended them, made the king of Persia favorable toward them, and provided them with prophets, such as Haggai and Zechariah, and with leaders, such as Zerubbabel, Ezra, and Nehemiah. True, the temple they had built was small, but God promised, "The glory of this present house will be greater than the glory of the former house," says the Lord Almighty. "And in this place I will grant peace," declares the Lord Almighty (Haggai 2:9).

All this had not satisfied them. They wanted more. They expected God to satisfy their expectations and to do so according to their time-table. When He acted according to His eternal plan, they responded by neglecting His worship, making light of His commandments, and seeking ways to satisfy themselves, even if it entailed disloyalty to the very covenant upon which they based their expectations.

Israel dared doubt God because they wanted everything at once as if they deserved anything at all. They dared doubt the love of God because of their daily hardships, which seemed to have greater weight than any-thing God had done in the past or promised for the future.

Like them, when faced with hardships, we are quick to distance our-selves from God. We doubt His goodness if our wishes are not satisfied at once. Somehow, we have forgotten that we do not deserve anything, and that life on earth of necessity involves pain, expectation, patient waiting, and difficulty because sin still surrounds us and dwells within us. We have forgotten how to endure. We want it all, now, at once, without cost, and without difficulty. We are greatly mistaken.

In times of crises, when we experience loss or impending danger, we are inclined to doubt the love of God and to forget evidences of His love for us. That is no way to treat Him who loved us so wonderfully. Those who have tasted of the Lord in the past and seen that He is good, whose sins have been forgiven because of the sacrifice of Christ, should be grateful all the more. We ought not measure God's love by the stan-dards of the world nor by those dictated by our impatience.

How did God respond to Israel's doubt? We would naturally expect Him to wipe such sinners off the face of the earth. But love is patient and kind. Love suffers all things and bears all things. Many waters can-not quench love—and God's love excels all other loves, known and un-known. God loves Israel. His love is not the product of Israel's capacities or achievements. It does not issue out of anything attributable to the people. So it was, and so it shall be because God is God. He is not caused, but causes all things. He is not shaped, but shapes all things according to the eternal perfection of His will. God's love is contingent upon noth-ing but His grace. That is what makes it so steady, so reliable. Heaven and earth will pass away, but the love of God will not be depleted by the smallest iota.

Israel had once again proven unworthy of God's love, but that cannot alter His love. He permitted Israel the terrible arrogance of its doubt, just as He permitted Job and Jeremiah to complain about His conduct of the world's affairs. He humbled Himself, allowed Himself to be called into account, and labored to persuade His miserable creatures of the reality of His love; He responded to their question, "How did you love us?" God's patience, the gentle kindness with which He treats us puny creatures, always surprises.

The Evidence of History

Israel asked, "How did You love us?" God replied: "was Esau not a brother to Jacob," says the Lord, "yet I loved Jacob and I hated Esau." Malachi goes back to the beginning of the nation's history, to the days of Isaac, Esau, and Jacob, described in Genesis 25:19–35:15. We cannot repeat the whole of that history here. You know the story well. Jacob, the youngest of the twins, was preferred by God over his brother. Before they were born, God determined, the older will serve the younger (Genesis 25:23).

This was a divine choice. It had nothing to do with Jacob's ancestry (Jacob and Esau shared the same father and mother). Nor was it the product of any action on Jacob or Esau's part (the two had not been born). Jacob was no better than Esau, certainly not while they in their mother's womb. Nevertheless, God chose to love Jacob and reject Esau. Grace, a love that is the product of God's heart, not of anything attributable to Jacob, is the source of that preference—just as my dear wife preferred me over far more worthy competitors. God's love is a love that flows from His goodness, from His grace. It is the opposite of merited goodwill.

We cannot attribute Jacob's preference to anything he would do in the future because most of his recorded actions were nefarious to the extreme. God confirmed the transfer of seniority from Esau to Jacob in spite of the devious methods Jacob used to secure it when he abused his brother's weakness and his father's trust (Genesis 25:27–34; 26:1–41). God's love did not find its rationale in what God foresaw that Jacob and Esau would do. Had this been the case, every sane person would have preferred Esau, in spite of his weakness, to the cunning, Machiavellian, cynical, and unscrupulous Jacob.

It is important to remember: we are not speaking of eternal destinies, but of matters that had to do with the here and now of this life. However, the principle is valid in all respects and with reference to anything God does. We cannot deny that God is master of His love. He loves whom He wishes to love and is not obliged to love any. In that sense, He has, at the least, the same measure of freedom that every man has in terms of the choice of his spouse, with the important difference that God is under no obligation to love any, nor has He a need to love any but Himself. We are under obligation to love all. Normal people cannot live without loving others.

God has the right to prefer one person and reject the other, to make covenant with one nation and leave the other nations in darkness, to love Jacob and hate Esau. No one can call Him into account for the choices He makes. No one can stand over God and demand that He justify His deeds. There is no measuring rod to which God is subject. He is His own standard, and His decisions are the product of His inherently righteous nature. They are right by virtue of the fact that He made them. There is no higher standard, no more worthy goal than God. He is the best of all things, the sum of all goodness.

Not only does God have such a right, but he exercises it. "Was Esau not a brother to Jacob," says the Lord, "yet I loved Jacob and I hated Esau." God preferred Jacob over Esau, so much so that, in comparison with His love to Jacob, His attitude toward Esau is one of hate. Here we must dare to be true to the Word of God, even when it is inconvenient: Malachi does not say that God's love to Jacob is so great that His love to Esau was like hatred. He says that God loved Jacob and hated Esau.

God is as much master of His hatred as He is of His love. Obviously, we all deserve to be hated by God. None are worthy of His love. All humans are sinful in His eyes. We have all earned His justified, holy, pure hatred. Jacob, the uninhibited liar, the miserable coward, was loved by God while still in his mother's womb. Esau, the man of action, was hated before he was born. Jacob, no more worthy than Esau, was loved.

Proof of God's discriminating love to Jacob is seen in the way He treated Israel in comparison with Edom. As to Edom, "I made his mountains a desolation and his inheritance the dwelling place of desert foxes." God gave Edom a portion of land southeast of the Jordan, in a dry and arid area, where desert foxes live. In Malachi's day, the Nabataeans had invaded Edom and conquered it. The Edomites had taken advantage of

Israel's absence from the land, fled their own land, and settled in the southern part of Judea. Malachi quotes the Edomites as saying, "we have been impoverished, but we will rebuild the ruins." By way of contrast, this is what the Lord of Hosts has said: "They will build—and I will destroy." Edom hoped for a national restoration: "we have been impoverished," that is to say, our land has been invaded, taken and destroyed, "but we will rebuild the ruins." Whose word, do you think, will prevail? Man never has the last word nor should he ever.

Edom declared its determined intention to return to the land and restore it, but, contrary to what was happening in Malachi's day to Israel, Edom would not succeed. Nothing can negate God's decree and no power can limit His power. Over against Edom's determination, Malachi sets God's holy, terrible determination. Over against Edom's puny strength, Malachi pits God's might. Edom might indeed rebuild, but God will destroy it all.

"And they will be called 'the land of wickedness' and 'the people with whom God is angry forever.'" Edom's fate will testify to its evil nature. Its punishment will be an ongoing witness to God's gracious love for Jacob and His holy, righteous hatred of Esau. It will display the undying faithfulness of that discriminatory love.

True, Jacob also was punished for his sin, but he, in the person of the returnees from Babylon, returned to his land after seventy years. What is more, God promised that the future was yet to be glorious. Edom's destruction, on the other hand, is final. There will be no restoration. The Edomites will be known as "the people with whom God is angry forever." Woe to those with whom God chooses to be angry forever!

The Grounds of Israel's Confidence

Because of God's mercies, Israel's fate was and remains secure. God did not forsake Israel in Malachi's time, in spite of Israel's unworthiness. He will not forsake them today. God does not choose nations or individuals for their worthiness. He chooses them by a grace that can never be stymied—a grace that is so sufficient that nothing is capable of severing the link God establishes by it.

That grace does not depend on a nation or an individual but on God, the giver of grace. God's stubborn, unmerited faithfulness to His people teaches us to be confident of God's grace to us in spite of our failures. God's faithfulness to the elect naturally and inevitably implies that He will be faithful to Israel, just as His treatment of Esau assures us of His eternal hatred of sin and of the horror of the fate awaiting those who refuse to forsake their sin.

Nothing can change God's faithfulness because it depends on nothing but God. He chose to relate to Esau in a way that was very different from the way He chose to relate to Jacob. Neither of them was worthy of God's attentions. Edom sinned against God frequently and was an enemy of both Israel and Judah over the years (Joel 3:16; Amos 1:6–11; Obadiah; Ezekiel 25). Israel also sinned by forsaking and perverting God's ways. Yet God punished Edom with a punishment that is to last forever; Israel He brought back to the land.

God acts in the same way to this day. None is worthy of His grace. Still, He shows mercy to some, although these "some" are as many as the sands on the shores of the sea, as many as the stars in heaven on which Abraham gazed. To the majority, He gives the just reward of their sins. Those redeemed in Christ are kept by the power of God for a salvation that is yet to be revealed (1 Peter 1:5). Nothing can separate them from the love of God. When they sin, He chastises them. But in so doing, He treats them as a father treats his children. The ground of our confidence is never in anything we do or are able to do. It is in the grace of God, which stands the tests of life and the doubts raised by our failures.

We should never think we are better than others because we were chosen. We should never think that God loves us because of some quality, ability, or action attributable to us. God loves those whom He loves in spite of their failings, and we are equals to the most miserable of mankind. We should never exalt ourselves above others. On the contrary, the grace of God toward us should motivate us to hope and work for the extension of such grace to others, however obvious it may be that they are unworthy.

And your eyes will see this, and you will say, "May the Lord be exalted beyond the borders of Israel." Malachi promised Israel that the day would come when they would see the punishment God will bring on Edom. They will then praise God for His grace and faithful love to them. Recognition of God's grace in contrast to the righteous anger that they deserve will motivate the people to long for Him to be glorified. They will aspire for His glory to extend beyond the borders of Israel, to the nations of the world.

God's special love to Israel distinguishes that nation among the nations and accords Israel a special position. We should not take this to mean that the other nations are doomed to utter darkness. The scope of Malachi's vision is wider than the people of Israel. He knows that Abraham was called to be the father of many nations (Genesis 17:4); that many nations are to be blessed through him (Genesis 12:3). For that reason, while Malachi is occupied with the sins of Israel, his heart is wide in expectation that the God of Israel will receive the honor that He deserves, and therefore He will be exalted beyond the borders of Israel.

Is that our vision? Do we, with Malachi, strive for the glory of God, longing that He would be exalted? If so, unlike Israel, we will not doubt His love in times of distress and will not limit our confidence in that love to days in which our selfish desires are met. If we love God because He first loved us, we will acknowledge the ways He showed us His love in the past and will not attribute anything to ourselves.

If we want God to be glorified, we will recognize His right to love and to hate as He wishes. We shall not measure Him by our standards or try to bind Him to our wishes. We will also not attribute more value to ourselves than the Scriptures justify. Malachi says the people of Israel will attribute to God the glory that He deserves because of what He will do. God's glory is the product of what God is and does. He glorifies Himself, and he does so, among other ways, by bringing the people of Israel to recognize and value His glory and to aspire that others, beyond their national borders, will do likewise.

LET'S SUMMARIZE:

1. God loves whom He wants to love. We should be grateful if we are among those He has graciously included in His love. If we do not know whether or not we are included, we should turn to God and ask to be included. God has promised never to reject those who turn to Him.

2. God's grace is the grounds and reason for our salvation. We cannot save ourselves, but God can save us to the uttermost.

3. Israel was not and is not worthy of God's grace. But the unfaithfulness of man cannot undo God's faithfulness. Israel will yet blossom and bud and fill the face of the earth with praise to God, simply because God is true though every man proves to be untrue.

4. Our salvation is dependent on God. That is why it is secure. We need not work for our salvation nor fear its loss. Our efforts are in response to our redemption, not a means to earn it.

5. God never hates any but those worthy of hatred. But He hates only those whom He wants to hate. That is His divine prerogative. We should avoid anything that is not pleasing to God.

6. Our desire should be that God would be glorified in Israel and in the world, in our families, and in our churches.

7. God will indeed glorify Himself. His glory does not depend on man but on Himself.

LET'S PRAY

Lord of Hosts,

You have given us life and,

by grace, distinguished us from other people:

The sun of Your righteousness

has shone on us with the light of Your only Son.

You lead us to eternal life.

Having redeemed us from the kingdom of darkness,

may it please You to ensure

that we constantly walk in the light of Your presence.

Guide us and grant us of Your goodness

so that we never stray

from the holy calling to which You have called us,

but continue faithfully

until we arrive at the goal You set before us.

Then, at long last, cleansed from the defilement of the flesh,

We shall be changed into the glorious image of Your only Son,

Jesus Christ our Savior.

Amen.

Questions for Discussion and Study

- What may we learn from this passage about God's independence in general and in His relations with man in particular?

- What can we learn from this passage about man's duties to God? What is the duty Malachi speaks of explicitly in this passage?

- Summarize what is said of Edom (the nation) in Scripture.

- What does Malachi teach us in this passage about God's activity in history?

- Compare what Malachi has to say in this passage with what Paul said in Ephesians 1.

CHAPTER 2

Where is My Honor?
(MALACHI 1:6–14)

"A son honors his father and a slave his master. And if I am a father, where is My honor? And if I am a master, where is My fear?" says the Lord of Hosts to you, the priests, despisers of My name. "And you say, 'In what way have we despised Your name?' You present disgusting food on my altar and you say, 'In what way have we despised Your name'! In your saying, 'The table of the Lord is despicable.'"

"And when you offer the blind for sacrifice, is that not evil? And when you offer the lame and the sick, is that not evil? Offer it to your governor—will he be pleased with you, will he accept you?" says the Lord of Hosts.

"'And now, please seek the face of God, that He might be merciful to us.' This is from your hand. Will He accept you?" says the Lord of Hosts. "Who among you will close the doors, that you do not light [a fire on] My altar for nothing. I have no interest in you," says the Lord of Hosts, "and a sacrifice I do not want from your hands, for from the rising of the sun and until its setting My name is great among the nations, and everywhere incense and a pure offering is offered to My name, for My name is great among the nations," says the Lord of Hosts.

"But you defile it by saying, 'the table of the Lord and its offerings are disgusting, His sacrifices are despicable.' And you say, 'here is a bothersome [matter]' and you snort at it," says the Lord of Hosts, "and you bring the stolen and the lame and the sick, and you bring the sacrifice—was I to receive it from your hand?" says the Lord. "Cursed is the deceiver who has in his herd a male, and he vows and sacrifices a faulty [animal] to the Lord, for I am a great king," says the Lord of Hosts, "and My name is dreadful among the nations."

Having spoken of God's love, the prophet speaks of it again from a different angle. There is no reason to believe that the prophecies of Malachi are arranged in chronological order. However, there is logic to the arrangement of the book. As we shall see, each portion leads to the next by the internal logic of their contents. This order was determined under inspiration of either the prophet or an unknown editor. It is possible that the connection between what we have seen and what we are about to see is precisely that to which I've pointed at the end of the first portion: we should respond to the love of God by longing for God to be honored as He deserves.

The fact that this book of prophesies may not have been edited by Malachi does not detract from its inspiration. This book, like every other book of the Bible, was written and arranged under the Spirit's inspiration so that we would be enabled to view it as a whole and identify the message. That message goes beyond the then-and-there of the words of the prophet, pointing us ever forward to an ever-more-clearer hope and longing that is yet to be fulfilled.

In the passage before us, God addresses the people (v. 1). But He does so through the priests (v. 6) because they were responsible for the conduct of the temple ritual and for teaching the people the ways of the Lord.

God Should Be Honored

God protests through the prophet. He begins by pointing out a commonplace truth: A son honors his father and a slave his master. There is a certain order in human society. Sons honor their fathers and slaves their masters. That is not how things always are, but that is how they should be. Deviations from the norm are departures from the natural order. Society cannot exist without structure, and structure cannot be functional in a constructive way unless sons honor their fathers and slaves their masters.

There is nothing inherently wrong with structure, although modern thinking often views structure as a limitation to be destroyed. Structure is for our good. Where anarchy reigns, none are responsible, none are accountable, and human society breaks down.

God has created us with an inherent need for structure. So it was in the Garden of Eden. God stood above all. His law was the guide of Adam and Eve's lives, informing them of their role in the world, according privileges, imposing duties, and setting necessary, protective boundaries within which they would be secure, free and happy.

Adam was appointed over the rest of the creatures, both animate and inanimate. He was to watch over them, tend them, and use them for God's appointed purposes. They were subject to Adam. Their welfare was his responsibility, and their fate was determined to a significant extent by his adhering to the structure God determined: Adam was to obey God and rule over creation.

Adam was created first. Eve was created for him, to be his complement, his friend, and his partner. Together, they were to rule creation for God. Disruption came when Adam, by eating of the tree God had forbidden him, overstepped the limitations.

So it is with Israel. God established Himself as their King and His Law as their guide. They were to love and honor Him by obeying Him. His Law informed them of their role in the world, accorded privileges, imposed duties, and set necessary boundaries within which they would be secure, free, and happy.

So it is with us. We too are appointed, guided, informed, blessed, warned, and our security, freedom, and happiness are protected by His Law, which is nothing less than a reflection of His eternal majesty. God is King of all mankind, and all are bound to love and honor Him. A son honors his father and slave his master. That is the order of things.

> "And if I am a father, where is My honor? And if I am a master, where is My fear?" says the Lord of Hosts to you, the priests, despisers of My name.

It is worth drawing attention to the two words used in this portion, *honor* and *fear*. Fear is not an attitude of craven humiliation nor is it the terror evoked by the presence of powerful evil. Fear of God is a combination of affectionate love and deep respect, joined to an awareness of majesty. One cannot honor God without lovingly respecting Him, without recognizing His glorious majesty. The fear of God is always affectionate. Love of God is always deeply respectful.

A son honors his father and a slave his master. God refers to moral assumptions that undergird human society, to the inherent moral obligation that is part of human nature: sons honor their fathers. Slaves honor their masters. It is right that it should be so, and all recognize this. Only in a corrupt, confused generation do children not honor their parents. Such a generation is in deep trouble. Woe to the family, congregation, society, or nation that does not teach, demand, and exemplify this principle.

Malachi is referring to the respect sons should have for their fathers. He does not excuse them from honoring their mothers. Fathers are mentioned because they are the head of the family. A son who does not respect his father will not respect his mother. Parental respect is one of the fundamentals of human society, one of the fundamental duties of mankind. That is why it is mentioned in the Ten Commandments: Honor your father and your mother, so that you may live long in the land the Lord your God is giving you (Exodus 20:12).

How do children honor their father? By their affectionate respect, gratitude, and obedience. The love of God imposes duties. A person who has been blessed by God is not free to live as he pleases. He must shape his life according to the will of God and to God's praise. He wants to do precisely that.

Such is the logic of the first commandment. In the Ten Commandments, God first establishes that it is He who blessed Israel and brought them out of Egypt. For that reason, the people are not free to worship other gods (I am the Lord your God, who brought you out of Egypt, out of the land of slavery. You shall have no other gods before Me, Exodus 20:2–3). Nor may Israel worship God in any way but that which He has commanded (You shall not make for yourself an image in the form of anything in heaven above or on the earth beneath or in the waters below. You shall not bow down to them or worship them, Exodus 20:4–5). A person who desires God to receive the honor He deserves will strive for that purpose. He will suit his life to God's commandments. Obedience is an important way to honor God. Individuals who do not obey Him do not honor Him.

The second principle issues out of the first: and a slave his master. Parental respect is at the foundation of society. It implies respect in all other contexts.

Malachi does not condone slavery any more than he speaks out against it. In ancient times, slavery was part of the fabric of civil society. The Torah transformed slavery by mitigating its nature: it protected slaves and accorded them rights. The Scriptures view slavery as a given. Only by implication do they lay the groundwork for the eventual destruction of that evil institution. Malachi simply states here that, as the world goes, slaves honor their masters. How do they do so? By showing them respect and obeying them.

God showed His faithful, fatherly love for Israel while teaching the people that He is the sovereign Creator and Ruler of the universe. God's kindness toward Israel should have given the people a reason to engage in His worship with joy as an expression of their gratitude.

Like them, we owe God a debt of gratitude and worship. Like them, we have learned that God is our heavenly Father, Lord of the universe, and sovereign of our lives. We too have received from God many expressions of kindness. Is our love for God warm? Does our worship burst out of a heart that is really and truly grateful?

The Priests Do Not Honor God

The priests would have to admit that their worship was far from appropriate. So God was forced to ask, "And if I am a father, where is My honor? And if I am a master, where is My fear?" says the Lord of Hosts to you, the priests, despisers of My name.

The priests did not honor God. They did not relate to Him as to a father and a master. They were responsible for the conduct of God's worship and for the implementation of the law of the covenant in the life of the nation. They were to teach the Israelites all the decrees the LORD has given them through Moses (**Leviticus 10:11**).

The nation was commanded to follow the priests' lead:

> If cases come before your courts that are too difficult for you to judge—whether bloodshed, lawsuits, or assaults—take them to the place the LORD your God will choose. Go to the Levitical priests and to the judge who is in office at that time. Inquire of them and they will give you the verdict.
>
> You must act according to the decisions they give you at the place the LORD will choose. Be careful to do everything they instruct you to do. Act according to whatever they teach you and the decisions they give you. Do not turn aside from what they tell you, to the right or to the left. Anyone who shows contempt for the judge or for the priest who stands ministering there to the LORD

your God is to be put to death. You must purge the evil from Israel
(Deuteronomy 17:8–12).

This was the priests' role. In Deuteronomy 33:8–10, which summa-
rizes the priests' tasks, teaching precedes sacrifice. That role became all
the more important with the absence of a temple, the consequent lack
of temple worship, and the need to provide the nation with a new point
of national adherence in pagan Babylon. At first, the priests rose to the
challenge. Gradually, a new spiritual leadership began to emerge consist-
ing largely of lay experts in the Law (these were the beginnings of the
rabbinical tradition). It is interesting to note that, in all his messages,
Malachi omits mention of the High Priest. This is especially interesting
in light of the High Priest's prominence among the returnees. However
important was the role the temple played in the nation's life, obviously
the priests played a lesser role than we might expect.

The priests in Malachi's day did not fulfill their obligations. Their
duty was especially important due to the fact that the returnees had no
king to rule over them. In many ways, they were in the same situation as
were their forefathers before they had requested a king. Yet the priests
did not fulfill this role.

Had the returnees responded to their circumstances by crowning
God over their lives, they would have honored God as He required of
their forefathers (1 Samuel 8:7; 10:18–19). They did not, and the priests
did not call the people to such a choice. They led the people, but not in
God's ways. So God turns to them in rebuke and describes them as despisers of My name.

Instead of bringing God honor, the priests dishonored Him. They did
not give Him the honor due Him as Father and Master nor did they teach
the people to do so. In our days, such a duty falls on the shoulders of
Pastors and Elders in the church and on parents in the family. If they are
to honor God, they must teach those under them the holiness of God,
His just demands, and their duties to Him. They must cultivate among
the people and in their families the fear of God, humility, honesty, and
faithfulness to God's Word. They must teach and exemplify how God
wishes to be worshipped. In spite of pressure from the world, they must
not compromise. They must maintain a steady godliness. If they do not,
they dishonor God as did the priests in Malachi's day.

Nowadays there is little difference between what is accepted in the
world and how many wish to worship God or conduct their family and
congregational lives. Pastors have become more like executives than

shepherds. Churches exist to meet the expectations of the people rather than to cultivate an eager, consistent spirituality. The words sung differ from those popular in the world (although they are similarly superficial, sometimes even more so). But the melodies, the behavior, the dress code, and the patterns of thought and action are almost identical to those embraced by the world around them.

We would do well to ask ourselves if we are honoring God or dishonoring Him. We would do well to examine ourselves: Are we fulfilling our role to be light and salt in the world, or have we lost so much of our light and our saltiness that we have nothing to offer those among whom we live?

The Priests Denied Their Guilt

The priests refused to accept Malachi's message: "On what grounds does Malachi accuse us of dishonoring God? What fault can he find in what we do? We serve in the temple. We bring sacrifices. That is what we were commanded to do. What else does he want?" And you say, "In what way have we despised Your name?"

God is not satisfied with mere sacrifices. Malachi responds in God's name, "You present disgusting food on My altar and you say, 'In what way have we despised Your name'! In your saying, 'The table of the LORD is despicable.' And when you offer the blind for sacrifice, is that not evil? And when you offer the lame and the sick, is that not evil? Offer it to your governor—will he be pleased with you? Will he accept you?" says the LORD of Hosts.

The priests allowed the people to make light of the worship of God and to bring unworthy sacrifices. Instead of leading the people in worship, they were led by the wishes of the people. They led "people friendly" temple worship. Such worship can never be "God friendly" because it is focused on the people and their wishes rather than on the glory of God and His commandments. It makes more of cultural, economic, and social circumstances than it does of the will of God. By such a means, it cultivates the opposite of biblical holiness. It substitutes troublesome godliness with a benign worldliness that has no character, no cutting edge, and no message.

Instead of insisting on the commandments of God, the priests found ways to soften God's demands. If the people would not bring the best of their harvest, herds, and flocks, whatever they agreed to bring would be sufficient. After all, those were difficult times. There was no need to be radical. There was room for compromise, for a bit of give and take—especially for a bit of take so long as we do the taking. After all, we should be happy they come to the temple at all and that they bring something with them. Imagine what would happen if they refused to bring sacrifices altogether!

God will respond to this idea later. He'll say that He'd rather have the doors of the temple closed than to allow the conduct of worship that does not involve the heart and is not the overflow of a loving fear of God. Such purported worship is, at best, a perfunctory execution of duty. Calvin is right in commenting at this point that nothing is dearer to God than His worship.

God demands the best. He has a right to more than the best. In mercy, He did not demand all that is rightly His. But Israel brought the poorest of its herds and flocks. They brought the animals for which they had little use—the blind, the lame, and the ill. The priests allowed them to do so.

God is not interested in our leftovers, in what we do not need, nor has He need of our best. Being God, He demands our best. He demands our honest love, all of our hearts, and all of our abilities. He demands the right to be first in our lives, the first of our priorities, primary to all our considerations.

Of course, the priests did not intend to dishonor God. They were engaged in His worship, were they not? But they lacked the fear of God which is so necessary in worship and especially among those who lead. As a result, they were not faithful to the word of God as is expected of those who serve in the house of God. Human considerations played too large a role in their choices, so they were ready to compromise. The lack of ill intent on their part was no excuse. "I didn't mean to" is an argument void of moral weight. Whether you intended or did not intend to do what you did, you are responsible. You might not have intended to injure someone when you pulled out of the driveway, but the consequences of your deed cannot be affected by your intention. We should be careful how we live and with what we say. We should ensure that our words and actions are better controlled by our intentions.

We dishonor God when we give Him the remnants of our time, resources, and strength. We dishonor God when we forgo prayer, serious study of the Bible, the cultivation of our spiritual life, or consistent church activity because we think we have something more important to do. We dishonor God when we prefer to watch a movie, spend time with friends, participate in sports, or chat at the expense of time we should be spending in the presence of God. I am not saying that those who fear the LORD should engage in nothing but spiritual exercises. What I am saying is that our spiritual exercises should be at the top of our list, not at the bottom.

Appealing to Conscience

God appeals to the priests' conscience: "And when you offer the blind for sacrifice, is that not evil? And when you offer the lame and the sick, is that not evil? Offer it to your governor—will he be pleased with you, will he accept you?" says the LORD of Hosts.

We know full well that God is not to be worshipped with defective offerings. That being so, Malachi asks, how can you even think of bringing such offerings to the temple? "When you offer the lame and the sick, is that not evil?" Malachi does not ask if such behavior is wise; he asks if it is not wrong to worship God in such a way. Is it not evil, even in the minds of those who choose to worship that way? God is appealing to the people's conscience. He is calling on them to examine their behavior and to condemn themselves. The priests obviously acted contrary to what they knew was right. There was a gap between the way they worshipped and their theoretical morality. There was therefore only one way to answer the questions Malachi had posited.

We are sometimes like the priests of Malachi's day. Like them, we know to do good, but prefer the lesser good—or even the evil, if they are attached to some kind of gain. Is it right to serve God in that way? "Offer it to your governor—will he be pleased with you, will he accept you?" says the LORD of Hosts.

The governor of Judea was appointed by the Persian king (Nehemiah 5:15) and served as his representative. Would the people dare bring him defective tribute? If they did, could they expect him to respond to their requests and receive them with kindness? Merely positing the question shows how unreasonable was the people's behavior.

Apparently, the priests had more regard for the Persian governor than they did for the glory of God. The governor's authority, his demands, and the punishments he was empowered to impose were more real in the minds of the returnees than God's demands, rights, and power. Do we never fail in a similar way, attributing greater weight to what our eyes see than to the spiritual, however eternal it may be? Do we honor men more than God? Do we seek to please men more than we seek to please God? Often, merely positing the question implies the answer. How about you?

One could make a case for the choices made by the people of Malachi's day: They had just arrived in the country. They needed to secure their future by ensuring that their sheep and cattle were healthy. This required the best of the flocks and the herds. It was only wise for them to expect the priests to compromise, and for them to winnow the blind, lame, and ill of the beasts by giving them to the temple for sacrifice. After all, God did not need the sacrifices. He also understood how much they needed the best of their animals at that stage of the nation's life.

God demanded the best, regardless of such considerations. He does the same today. There is always a good reason to give God the remnants of our resources while we retain the best: we have to pay for schooling, buy a car, repair our car, marry off a daughter, or take that vacation. But God is not prepared to accept sacrifices that cost us nothing. He demands of us to make Him first in our priorities. There is no room for the kind of compromises the returnees chose to make, any more than there is for our poor choices. God demands that we honor Him by denying ourselves daily. He demands the right to be loved more than we love our fathers, mothers, brothers, sisters, or anything in this world. He is unwilling to receive our lame and blind offerings.

No one has ever lost by sacrificing for God. Remember Jim Elliot's pithy statement: "He is no fool who gives what he cannot keep to gain what he cannot lose." God's blessings always exceed anything we are able to sacrifice. But He is not willing to play second fiddle. He demands the first place in our preferences and our loves.

How generous are *we* in *our* offerings to the church? How careful are we not to give too much, lest we will not be able to buy the next toy upon which we have set our heart? To what extent can we say that what we give to God is a sacrifice rather than a halfhearted conceding of surplus? How well do our spiritual leaders teach us to sacrifice for God, to give Him our best and our utmost? How well do they exemplify that sacrifice in their lives?

And now, please seek the face of God, that He might be merciful to us. The Hebrew is difficult at this point. It seems like Malachi is mocking the people by quoting them as they bring their defective sacrifices to the temple and request of the priests to pray that God would be merciful to them. Some interpreters believe they see in the wording of the people's request a reflection of the Aaronic blessing (Numbers 6:23–25). There are undeniable verbal similarities: face of God, merciful to us. These interpreters might be right. In any case, it does not change the meaning of the words.

"This is from your hand. Will He accept you?" says the LORD of Hosts. These are probably the words of the LORD to the priests: This (these sacrifices) is what you bring to God (is from your hand). Do you think it reasonable to expect that He accept you? says the LORD of Hosts. Should He, in response to your offerings, acknowledge you, give you audience, and grant your requests? Again, the answer is obvious. T. V. Moore says in this context, "God will not despise the widow's mite, but He will certainly despise the miser's." This appeal to reason sharpens the question and transforms it into a means geared to awaken a sleepy conscience.

It Would Be Better to Close the Temple's Doors

"Also, who among you will close the doors, that you do not light [a fire on] My altar for nothing. I have no interest in you," says the LORD of Hosts, "and a sacrifice I do not want from your hands." The paragraph begins with the word *also*, that is to say, "what is more." What follows is over and above what God has said so far about Israel's false worship. He would rather that one of the priests (who among you) draw the logical conclusion and, instead of acting as if all is well, use his authority to bring an end to the sham of worship.

Instead of the paltry kind of worship in which the people were involved, it would be better to close the doors of the temple and extinguish the fire on the altar. Israel's worship of God is for nothing because it has no value and will bring none of the desired results. God is calling on the priests to display a holy concern for His honor and end the display in which the people engaged, masqueraded as worship. No one responded to that call. There were no zealots among the priests, none who cared enough for God's honor.

In light of the efforts the returnees invested in reconstructing the temple and of the great expectations they had in connection with the renewal of God's worship, these are stringent words. "I have no interest in you," says the LORD of Hosts, "and a sacrifice I do not want from your hands." Your halfhearted worship is an expression of extreme scorn, however unintended, says the Lord. I therefore do not want you and do not want your offerings.

In today's terms, it is better to drop all pretense and stay home than to be satisfied with attending church merely to go through the motions. It is better not to claim to be Christian than to love God halfheartedly. It is better not to do any of the many things we do as Christians unless we do them with devotion, with an enthusiasm that is born out of honest gratitude for what God has done for us. Our actions should issue out of a gladly embraced duty to serve God faithfully. All too many times in the course of Israel's history, the people were satisfied with the ritual of God's worship, neglecting its heart. They worshipped Him outwardly, but their hearts were far from Him. Woe to us if we behave as they did.

God is Adored the World Over

If we refuse to learn the lesson, if we seek to satisfy ourselves by noncommittal, religious action, God will say to us as He did to Israel in Malachi's day, "Also, who among you will close the doors, that you do not light [a fire on] My altar for nothing. I have no interest in you," says the LORD of Hosts, "and a sacrifice I do not want from your hands, for from the rising of the sun and until its setting My name is great among the nations, and everywhere incense and a pure offering is offered to My name, for My name is great among the nations," says the LORD of Hosts. I have no need of your sacrifices. I have no need for you to worship Me. I have no need of the temple. These are all for you, not for Me.

Why "I have no need"? God is not pointing here to His lack of dependence on man, nor is He referring to His eternally self-sufficient character. Of course He is not dependent on man. Of course He is eternally self-sufficient. But here He is speaking of something over which many stumble, as they did in the days of the apostles: You dishonor My name, says God, but from the rising of the sun and until its setting My name is great among the nations. You bring Me unworthy offerings, but everywhere incense and a pure offering is offered to My name.

How is this possible? Does God reject Israel's ritually faithful but halfhearted worship and accept the idolatrous worship of the nations? Of course not. The Scriptures frequently and clearly affirm that idolatrous practices are hateful to God.

Is He referring to Israel's dispersion, worshipping God among the nations? Israel was indeed dispersed at that time throughout the ancient Far East, with some settling as far as the regions now known as India and Afghanistan. Others settled as far to the west as Spain. It is possible that

God is referring to that dispersion, in which case He would be saying that He did not need to be worshipped at the temple. There are Jews worshipping and honoring Him from the rising of the sun and until its setting. In other words, "don't think yourself so important and don't overestimate the value of your resettling the land and rebuilding the temple. I can manage quite well without you."

On the other hand, it is possible that God is referring here to Gentiles among the nations, who had heard of Him and learned to fear Him. We hear of the fear of God and of offering sacrifices to God by the pagan sailors who shared ship with Jonah (Jonah 1:16. See also 2 Kings 5:15–19; Daniel 4:31–34).

Both explanations face the difficulty involved in assuming that sacrifices were offered to the LORD in various places of the world on a regular basis (which is what is implied in the terms Malachi uses), and that incense and a pure offering are brought to the Lord. According to the Law, such offerings could be made only in the temple.

In Thebes, a city in Egypt, the Judean exiles had established a temple, but this temple never received divine sanction and certainly could not replace the temple in Jerusalem. God had explicitly commanded that offerings to Him be made nowhere else but in the Jerusalem temple. It is therefore unlikely that the LORD is referring to this temple. If He were, it would not be possible to speak of it as from the rising of the sun and until its setting.

There is no way to determine conclusively what the LORD meant by these statements. What is clear is that the God intended to make it clear that He derived no pleasure in the miserable sacrifices the people brought. His name and His greatness were adored among the nations from one end of the earth to another, yet the returnees continued to bring defective sacrifices.

God is not dependent on the temple, on Israel's worship, or on anything the priests are capable of doing for Him. His greatness is not limited to them and to their recognition.

The priests, on the other hand, defile His name. How? "By saying, the table of the LORD and its offerings are disgusting, His sacrifices are despicable. And you say, 'here is a bothersome [matter],' and you snort at it," says the LORD of Hosts, "and you bring the stolen and the lame and the sick, and you bring the sacrifice—will I receive it from your hand?" says the Lord.

Of course, the LORD is not quoting what the priests actually said. He is referring to the implications of what they did. As the saying goes, "actions speak louder than words." By agreeing to offer the kind of offerings brought to the temple, they were defiling the temple of the LORD and His altar (for the reference to the table of the Lord, see Ezekiel 41:22; 44:16 and compare with 1 Corinthians 10:21. Like Malachi, Paul speaks of judgment due to participants making light of the meaning of the ceremony). They were treating the altar like one would treat something disgusting and His sacrifices as something despicable.

They were, in fact, acting in direct contradiction to the Law, which states, If an animal has a defect, is lame, blind, or has any serious flaw, you must not sacrifice it to the LORD your God (Deuteronomy 15:21). Offerings were to be flawless (Leviticus 3:1, 6; 4:3, 32; and many others). By presenting faulty, worthless offerings, the priests and the people showed that they considered the worship of God bothersome. It caused them to snort at it while engaged in the rituals, waiting for the moment they ended so they could return to work or play.

Do none among us treat God's worship in a similar way? Do we sometimes come to church unwillingly and listen to the sermon with discreet but determined disinterest? Do we glance from time to time at our watches: "When on earth is this going to end?"

"From the rising of the sun and until its setting My name is great among the nations, and everywhere incense and a pure offering is offered to My name, for My name is great among the nations" says the LORD of Hosts. Which is why the LORD asks, "You bring the stolen and the lame and the sick, and you bring the sacrifice—will I receive it from your hand?" The people not only brought worthless sacrifices, which the priests allowed, but the people even brought the stolen. That is to say, offerings stolen from others! Can we imagine God would be satisfied with such offerings?

A Curse on the Deceivers

Malachi provides an immediate answer: "Cursed is the deceiver who has in his herd a male, and he vows and sacrifices a faulty [animal] to the Lord, for I am a great king," says the LORD of Hosts, "and My name is dreadful among the nations."

People in need are willing to promise almost anything. They will vow to the Lord, "God, if you but heal my wife, give me that job, if you but do this or that for me ... I will do this and that for you." At such a moment, they are willing to make extravagant promises. Afterward, when God grants them their wish, they seek ways to reduce the burden of their undertaking. "I have a male in my flock, but I need him, and males are worth a lot. Why be over-pedantic? What does it matter if I bring a female?" So we bring a female or a faulty [animal]. Whoever does that is cursed by the Lord. Cursed is the deceiver who has in his herd a male, and he vows and sacrifices a faulty [animal] to the Lord.

God is worthy of more. He demands more, and He insists that He receive more. Whoever does not serve the LORD from the heart is a deceiver, stealing from God. He is a deceiver, presenting himself as if he loves and worships God while his heart is given to other things. That is why he is also cursed. It is the duty of every human to worship God. It is certainly the duty of every Israelite, and of all who have been the recipients of His saving grace. Whoever does not worship Him is "cursed, for I am a great king," says the LORD of Hosts "and My name is dreadful among the nations."

God's greatness obliges us to worship Him from the heart, to love Him sincerely, to serve Him with an honest enthusiasm, in gratitude because we recognize His goodness, and with a faithfulness that recognizes its duty before Him. He is a great King, greater than all others. If we acknowledge His greatness, we shall worship Him appropriately. His name is dreadful among the nations. If we acknowledge His beautiful horror, loving fear will characterize our behavior at church and the way we worship Him.

It is not the "in" thing to think in such terms. Malachi was not concerned with accommodating himself to the latest expectations of his generation. We should learn from him. He swam against the stream. If we consider faithfulness to God more important than popularity with our peers, we will also need to swim in that direction.

LET'S SUMMARIZE:

1. We are obliged to honor God by respecting, loving, and obeying Him. That obligation is also a sweet privilege.

2. God greatly esteems the way we worship Him: Do we worship from the heart? Are we enthusiastic about His worship? Or are we performing a ritual that does not involve our hearts?

3. We must give God our best in terms of time, resources, and abilities. To that end, we must deny ourselves daily and love Him above all else.

4. God's glory is revealed and His will is done in highly unexpected circumstances. God is not dependent upon His people or upon what they do.

Let's Pray

Almighty God,

You are worthy of our love, respect, and obedience,

yet we are slow, often unwilling, to give what You deserve.

Teach us by Your Word, and move us by Your Spirit

to love You enthusiastically.

Never allow us to engage in mere ritual.

May all we do ever be directed at Your glory and by Your Word.

May we love You beyond all loves and trust You in all situations,

that Your honor might spread over all the earth

and Your will be done on earth

as it is done in heaven.

By the grace of Your Son and the power of Your Spirit,

through whom we pray.

Amen.

Questions for Discussion and Study

- Discuss various orders of society: Describe their structure, indicating their value and their limits.

- Define and describe worship that is acceptable to God. Be sure to base your conclusions on Scripture.

- Identify ways we try to reduce the level of our commitment and define biblical answers to such attempts.

- Describe the family structure as inferred in this chapter. Is this structure valid today and to what extent does it fit reality in our society?

- How does love oblige the lover, and what duties does it impose?

- Describe similarities and differences between the roles of the priests in the temple and those of pastors and elders today.

- Is there room for formality and ritual in the worship of God today? If there is, what is its value and what are its dangers?

- Compare the circumstances in which the returnees found themselves with those of new immigrants, new couples, and those just introduced to the job market. Do not forget to include a description of their mistaken assumptions.

CHAPTER 3

The Covenant with Levi
(MALACHI 2:1–9)

"And now, this commandment is for you, priests: If you do not hear and if you do not apply your hearts to honoring My name," says the LORD of Hosts, "I will cast the curse on you, and I will curse your blessings, I will surely curse them because you do not apply your heart. I will curse your seed and spread offal on your faces, the offal of your celebratory [offerings] and carry you to it. And you will know that I have cast this message on you, that My covenant will be with Levi," says the LORD of Hosts.

"My covenant was with him, [promising] life and peace, and I gave him My fear and he feared Me and he trembled at My name. True teaching was in his mouth and wickedness was not found on his lips. In peace and honesty he walked with Me, and many he turned from iniquity. For the lips of a priest preserve knowledge, and the Law is sought from his mouth because he is a messenger of the LORD of Hosts.

"But you have strayed from the way, you have caused many to stumble at the Law, you have corrupted the covenant of Levi," says the LORD of Hosts. "And I have also made you to be despised and worthless [in the mind] of all the people, even as you do not keep My ways and are partial in [applying] the Law."

The previous section spoke of the priests as representatives of the people. This section reiterates the theme from a slightly different angle. Do not be surprised when we return to the same subjects with a slight difference. We are but following Malachi's train of thought. There is an inner logic to the arrangement of this book, as there is to all the books of the Bible.

Previously, the prophet discussed the priests' attitude toward the worship of God, with special regard to the sacrifices. Here his rebuke focuses primarily on the fact that the priests were unfaithful to the covenant God made with the tribe of Levi when He brought the people out of Egypt. The priests, the son of Levi, were unfaithful to the covenant. But God will be faithful. He will therefore bring onto the priests the punishments promised by the covenant to those who transgress it.

God will Curse the Blessings

The words and now do not indicate a time but serve to strengthen the force of the statement. This commandment is for you, priests. The commandment to which Malachi refers is the duty imposed in what follows, a duty fully compatible both with the covenant God made with the priests (all of whom came from the tribe of Levi) and with the threat that accompanied that covenant. It is directed at you, priests.

The earlier message was addressed to the people and, by extrapolation, to the priests because they were to lead the people in matters relating to the worship of God and to the conduct of their lives. All who are appointed to the worship of God and over the lives of believers bear, by virtue of their task, a heavy responsibility. They must ensure that lives and worship are based on the Word of God, properly understood and applied.

As we said earlier, the worship of God is not meant for the enjoyment of the worshippers but for the honor and glory of God. God forbade worship by means that were common among the nations of the time. You shall not make for yourself an image in the form of anything in heaven above or on the earth beneath or in the waters below. You shall not bow down to them or worship them; for I, the LORD your God, am a jealous God (Exodus 20:4–5). He demanded pure, faultless sacrifices. He commanded when, how, and where He was to be worshipped. The priests were not at liberty to determine these matters in light of circumstances.

By allowing the people to bring defective offerings, the priests were cooperating with them in framing the terms of their worship, much as did Aaron when he acceded to the people's demand and created the golden calf. The priests' guilt was rooted in that cooperation. They were required to refuse faulty sacrifices. God's worship is so important that He provided the priests with clear instructions as to what was and what was not permitted.

How we worship God deeply impacts the way we think of Him. A defective practice distorts our understanding. In the long run, if we worship Him wrongly, we end up thinking of Him wrongly. That is why Israel was forbidden to use common methods in the worship of Jehovah. That is also why the church should be careful to guide its worship by the explicit commandments of God, adding nothing and doing nothing less.

God is not to be worshipped in any way but as He has commanded. True, the liberty we enjoy in this matter is broader than accorded our forefathers, but limits are still limits. We must shape our worship for His pleasure, for His honor, and according to the principles of His Word. We must not love ourselves in our worship. We must not be influenced by concepts borrowed from the world, let alone in terms framed by other religions, be they Muslim, Buddhist, or Jewish. There is no room to introduce into the worship of God incense, Torah scrolls, the lighting of candles, icons, banners, acting, or prayer shawls.

We saw that the people were preoccupied with the difficulties and economic challenges of the day. These led them to moderate their devotion to God. The priests acceded to such compromises. We are not at liberty to follow their example and compromise with regard to devotion to God. He must be our first priority at all times. This is true with regard to the conduct of church life, including congregational worship. Those who lead in the church are particularly responsible. That is why God said, This commandment is for you, priests.

What, then, is the commandment? Here it is:

> "If you do not hear and if you do not apply your hearts to honoring My name," says the LORD of Hosts, "I will cast the curse on you, and I will curse your blessings, I will surely curse them because you do not apply your heart. I will curse your seed and spread offal on your faces, the offal of your celebratory [offerings] and carry you to it. And you will know that I have cast this message to you, that My covenant will be with Levi," says the LORD of Hosts.

The commandment is a warning. You must apply your hearts to honoring Me. If you do not, I will turn even the blessings you have from Me into curses. I will humiliate and shame you. Your fate will be the fate of the offal from the sacrifices you are offering. You will know that all this came from Me in accordance with the covenant I made with the house of Levi. You are breaking covenant in the way you conduct my worship. I will keep covenant in the punishments I will bring upon you.

As when Jonah was sent to Nineveh (In forty days Nineveh will be overturned! Jonah 3:4), the threat was meant to bring the priests to repentance and thus spare them the threatened punishments. The message is an act of grace, a call to turn from the wrong way.

"If you do not hear, and if you do not apply your hearts to honoring My name," says the LORD of Hosts. That was the role of the priests, to honor My name. That was also their great privilege. In a special way, we all have our callings. Not everyone was permitted to conduct God's worship in the temple. Not everyone may conduct worship in the church. There were twelve tribes in Israel, and only one was chosen for the task. There were many families in the tribe of Levi, but only Aaron's family was chosen for the priesthood.

This was a great honor. It implied great responsibility. There might be room for us to reconsider the modern practice of asking people to lead in worship, simply because they are musically inclined (as if music is the main means of worship). I daresay that, nowadays, we have too much music and too little biblical understanding in our worship.

God Is to Be Worshipped Carefully

In the previous chapter, Malachi insisted that the priests dishonored God by the way they conducted the temple services. They dishonored God by taking the people's wishes into account (say *that* to a modern congregation!). They conceded to the natural selfishness that pulsates in the heart of every human by allowing the returnees to bring cheap, unworthy offerings rather than their best, as the Law commanded. They took the liberty to change the commandments of God and permitted the people to worship halfheartedly.

God responds to this by saying, "If you do not hear, and if you do not apply your hearts to honoring My name," says the LORD of Hosts, "I will cast the curse on you, and I will curse your blessings, I will surely curse them because you do not apply your heart."

We must apply our hearts to the worship of God. We must worship Him carefully, fearfully. Our God is a consuming fire, the terror of angels and the object of their loving adoration. When He revealed Himself to people, they were gripped with a sense of awful fear. He is called the Terror of Isaac (Genesis 31:42). When Isaiah saw the hem of His garments, he cried out, Woe to me! I am ruined! For I am a man of unclean lips, and I live among a people of unclean lips, and my eyes have seen the King, the

LORD Almighty (Isaiah 6:5). **The book of Psalms is full of testimonies to** His frightening greatness:

> The LORD reigns, let the nations tremble;
> He sits enthroned between the cherubim, let the earth shake.
> Great is the LORD in Zion; He is exalted over all the nations.
> Let them praise your great and awesome name—He is holy.
> The King is mighty, He loves justice—You have established equity;
> in Jacob You have done what is just and right.
> Exalt the LORD our God and worship at His footstool; He is holy.
> Moses and Aaron were among His priests,
> Samuel was among those who called on His name;
> they called on the LORD and He answered them.
> He spoke to them from the pillar of cloud;
> they kept His statutes and the decrees He gave them.
> Lord our God, You answered them;
> You were to Israel a forgiving God,
> though You punished their misdeeds.
> Exalt the LORD our God and worship at His holy mountain,
> for the LORD our God is holy (**Psalm 99**).

God threatens to curse all who refuse to honor Him. He threatens to curse all who will not apply their hearts in worship. Do we apply our hearts when we come to church? Do we apply our hearts to what we sing, to the prayers, to the sermon? Or do we come, fill a space while our mind wanders during the sermon, sing a bit, doze during prayer—and go home?

> "If you do not apply your hearts to honoring My name," says the LORD of Hosts, "I will cast the curse on you, and I will curse your blessings, I will surely curse them because you do not apply your heart. I will curse your seed and spread offal on your faces, the offal of your celebratory [offerings] and carry you to it."

These are harsh words. The word I have translated, cast, is especially hard. In context, the Hebrew connotes a combination of forcefully casting something negative on someone (flinging it), and of forcefully sending something to someone (imposing it). In other contexts, it can infer a positive act, such as forcefully extracting Israel from Egypt. But it is always a forceful act. However harsh, we need to hear what is said because it is in the Word of God. God's Word includes more than hugs and kisses. The Scripture contains rebuke and piercing calls to change our ways.

God threatens, if the priests will not heed the divine message Malachi was commissioned to bring; He will fling the curse on them. The term curse is also a harsh term. It is not the usual one used to describe a curse. The prophet is quoting the covenant:

> If you do not obey the LORD your God and do not carefully follow all His commands and decrees I am giving you today, all these curses will come on you and overtake you: You will be cursed in the city and cursed in the country. Your basket and your kneading trough will be cursed. The fruit of your womb will be cursed, and the crops of your land, and the calves of your herds and the lambs of your flocks. You will be cursed when you come in and cursed when you go out. The LORD will send on you curses ... (**Deuteronomy 28:15–20**).

In all cases in which the term curse appears in the above text, the same Hebrew word is used, and it is identical to that used by Malachi.

Paul writes to the Corinthians in the same vein with regard to the communion (the Lord's Table):

> Whenever you eat this bread and drink this cup, you proclaim the Lord's death until He comes. So then, whoever eats the bread or drinks the cup of the Lord in an unworthy manner will be guilty of sinning against the body and blood of the Lord. Everyone ought to examine themselves before they eat of the bread and drink from the cup. For those who eat and drink without discerning the body of Christ eat and drink judgment on themselves. That is why many among you are weak and sick, and a number of you have fallen asleep (**1 Corinthians 11:26–30**).

I will cast the curse on you, and I will curse your blessings, I will surely curse them because you do not apply your heart. **To which blessings is the LORD referring? To the blessings of the fields and the flocks, the herds and the families.** The people's physical resources were given them by God. Did they recognize that? Do we recognize that our employment and our homes, our family and our lives, the clothes we wear and the food on our tables are blessings from God? Do we treat them as blessings or take them for granted?

I will curse your blessings means that God would take from the people what He gave them. Instead of crops, what they sowed would die in the field. Instead of milk, the udders of the sheep and the cattle would shrivel. Their children would be diseased. Why? Because you do not apply your heart as you worship. Beware, dear friends, be very careful how you worship!

God says further that if Israel does not apply its heart to worship, I will curse your seed and spread offal on your faces, the offal of your celebratory [offerings] and carry you to it. God's anger is evident in the way the words are framed. When God is angry, who can withstand Him? He will not only curse our seed, but He threatens to spread the offal of the sacrificial animals on the faces of those who worship Him halfheartedly. The offal are in the inward parts of an animal—the inedible parts that God had commanded to burn outside the camp because they were unclean (see, for example, Exodus 29:14; Leviticus 4:11; 8:18; 16:27; Numbers 19:5). This included the dung and whatever was in the beasts' belly. God threatens to show His anger by spreading these disgusting parts, blood and all, on the faces of the priests who worshipped and allowed Him to be worshipped halfheartedly. They would be shamed and defiled.

As if that were not enough, God further threatens, I will ... carry you to it. What is the "it" to which the unfaithful priests are to be carried, and what does it mean to be carried to "it"? While the syntax is strange, the context clarifies the meaning. "It" is the offal, just mentioned. We've seen that these unclean parts of the sacrificial animals were taken outside the camp to be destroyed. It seems that what God is saying here is that he will have the priests carried out with the offal and treated as it was treated. These are frightening words. The punishment equals the weight of responsibility which the priests carried. It is to that responsibility that God next refers.

"And you will know that I have cast this message on you, that My covenant will be with Levi," says the LORD of Hosts. When I treat you in this way, you will know that it is Me, the LORD of Hosts, who has done this to you. I sent Malachi with the warning, and I fulfilled the terms of the covenant with Levi. You have broken covenant; I will keep it by bringing upon you the punishments dictated therein.

How Should a Prophet Function?

God reminds the priests of the covenant: My covenant was with him, that is to say, with Levi. Of course, the reference is to the family of Aaron within the tribe of Levi. The covenant promised Aaron and his family life and peace. God said to Phinehas, the son of Aaron, Behold, I give unto him my covenant of peace: and he shall have it, and his seed after him, even the covenant of an everlasting priesthood (Numbers 25:12–13).

Phinehas inherited his father's position as High Priest. God reminds the priests of Malachi's day what He had promised Phinehas if he and his descendants were true to their covenantal duties: life and peace. The worship of God draws worshippers closer to Him, reminding them who He is and what He is like. This intimacy is life: abundant, satisfying, pure, and wonderful. It is a peace that exceeds human logic and understanding. The psalmist says, You make known to me the path of life; You will fill me with joy in Your presence, with eternal pleasures at Your right hand (Psalm 16:11). No blessing, no happiness, no life is more wonderful than the reality produced by true worship of God.

And I gave him My fear. Not only did I teach him, says the Lord, but I worked secretly in his heart and planted my fear there. God works in our hearts as we worship Him. Phinehas, says God, responded to that work, feared Me and he trembled at My name. We are not robots. We are humans, created in the image of God and called to respond to the gracious workings of God in our lives and hearts. If we relate to Him with the fear that He planted in our hearts, we will be blessed.

There is room for fear in our worship. There is room for a lively recognition of the majesty of God's holiness, of His amazing power, of His astounding, disturbing, attractive eternity. There is room for us to tremble in His presence (he trembled at My name). "There is room," I said? It would be more apropos if I said, "there is need." Where no fear of God is to be found, there is no recognition of His greatness. Worship becomes a form of entertainment, just as Christian sing-alongs and concerts are often described nowadays as "worship" events. In many cases, there is no real adoration of God, only an enjoyment of music with scant reference to the words. We are often willing to sing theological and literary nonsense so long as the music appeals to our senses.

Similarly, the highest compliment we often give the preacher is "I really enjoyed that." We come to church to enjoy ourselves. We prefer to be entertained by comfortable seats, soothing voices, nice singing, good music, and encouraging preaching rather than be called to repentance. "If you do not apply your hearts to honoring My name," says the LORD of Hosts, "I will cast the curse on you, and I will curse your blessings, I will surely curse them because you do not apply your heart. I will curse your seed and spread offal on your faces, the offal of your celebratory [offerings] and carry you to it."

When a priest feared the Lord, true teaching was in his mouth. Why? We've already said that the way we worship God impacts the way we think of Him. If we worship Him according to His commandments, in sincere fear and with all our heart, of us too it will be said, true teaching was in his mouth. Biblical worship cultivates thinking that is true to God's Word. It protects us against deviations in terms of how we think (true teaching was in his mouth) as well as how we live (and wickedness was not found on his lips).

A person who fears God is careful in matters of honesty and truth. He conducts himself with integrity. He understands that God's holiness obliges him to holiness and that the righteousness of God obliges him to be honest, fair, generous, humble, kind, considerate, courageous, and faithful. He understands that it is not enough to participate in temple services. Day-to-day conduct is required, and he endeavors to live up to those requirements.

Such a person cultivates the presence of God and seeks His continuous blessing: In peace and honesty he walked with Me. He walks with God. His life is lived out in God's company. He serves God as God should be served (in honesty regarding God's Word) and enjoys peace in His presence.

As a result, many he turned from iniquity. Not by distributing tracts or making pronouncements but by his attractive, captivating holiness, which endears him even to the worst, persuading them intellectually, and motivating them to want to be like him. It is difficult to find anything more heartwarming, more beautifully human than a person who loves God and conducts himself with humble purity. It is hard to find anything more persuasive than the truth of God lived out by a godly individual. Small wonder that such a person turns many from iniquity.

Do we want to be like that? Do we want to honor God? Do we want our light to shine before people in such a way that they will be drawn to glorify our Father who is in heaven?

People who describe themselves as Christians and whose lives are not pure are traitors to themselves, to their professed faith, and to God. If we live on the threshold, without conceding to the world and without letting it go, if we compromise our conscience, if we conduct ourselves dishonestly and without holiness, if we are selfish, bitter, and unhappy with our circumstances, we are the opposite of what we ought to be. Instead of inspiring examples that command respect, we exemplify compromising hypocrisy of the kind that evokes contempt.

The lips of a priest preserve knowledge, and the Law is sought from his mouth because he is a messenger of the LORD of Hosts. That is the priest's role. He is called to preserve and teach knowledge and to be the kind of person that the Law is sought from his mouth because he fears God, knows the Scriptures, and has the courage to tell people the truth, even when it is unpleasant and unwelcome.

When a priest is faithful to his calling, he is a messenger of the LORD of Hosts. He addresses the people with the word of the Lord. He is not at liberty to speak from his heart, just as he is not at liberty to lead the people in the direction they choose. He faithfully teaches what is in the Law of the Lord. That was the priests' role and that is the role of all Christians, especially those in leadership positions in society, the home, and at church.

Did the priests meet those obligations? But you, Malachi says. You were supposed to be faithful but you have strayed from the way instead of leading in it. You strayed a little here and a little there. Even a ten-thousand-mile walk begins with the first step, and you took it—in the wrong direction.

As a result, instead of being a guide to the perplexed and an example to others, you have caused many to stumble at the Law. You have not only sinned but caused others to sin. Instead of being positive, your influence was baneful. Others saw how the priests conducted themselves and said, "If that is what fearing God means, I prefer not to fear Him." They turned to you for advice, and you guided them into a convoluted path. "You have corrupted the covenant of Levi," says the LORD of Hosts. You transgressed the covenant. In response, I have also made you to be despised and worthless [in the mind] of all the people. I exposed your shame in the sight of the nation. Why? Because you do not keep My ways and are partial in [applying] the Law.

Non-Kosher Preferences

This last accusation is worthy of closer examination. What does it mean to be partial in applying the Law? In context, it means that, when asked to determine how the Law is to be applied in a given situation, you take into account the social status of the person concerned and his ability to forward or impede your interests.

The priests were dependent upon the people. A major source of their livelihood was to come from sacrifices brought by them. So, the priests did not ask themselves, what does God's Word say? They made a simple calculation: It is better for the people to bring defective sacrifices than that they bring none at all— the opposite of God's view. He already said that He prefers the doors of the temple to be shut rather than to be worshipped in the faulty, halfhearted way in which the people worshipped Him in Malachi's time.

Why did the priests think in such terms? Because the sacrifices were an important source of income—"A man's gotta make a living, doesn't he?" The answer is simple: No, not necessarily. It is better to be penniless; it is better to die than to dishonor the Lord. Now, *that* was an idea the priests never entertained. Do we? Does God have the right to demand that we love Him more than we love pleasures or life? Do we recognize that right?

There was a time when Christians were glad to die for the honor of God. There was a time when the faithful faced jeers, flogging, chains, and imprisonment. They were put to death by stoning; they were sawed in two; they were killed by the sword. They went about in sheepskins and goatskins, destitute, persecuted, and mistreated—the world was not worthy of them. They wandered in deserts and mountains, living in caves and in holes in the ground (Hebrews 11:36–38). Yet they considered such suffering not worthy to be compared with the glory that would later be revealed in them.

The world is worthy of the kind of Christians it has. God is not. The question is, dare we, *will* we be different? Dare we love God with all our heart, soul, and strength? Dare we view the pleasures of the world as no more than dung compared to the privilege of being found in Him?

Let's Summarize

1. Spiritual leadership imposes spiritual responsibility. We would be wise not to seek leadership positions and to be very careful when we fill such roles.

2. Spiritual leadership is primarily a matter of faithfully living by and teaching God's Word. We should focus on and measure those who wish to lead us.

3. God is to be worshipped carefully, according to His commandments, not to our wishes, comfort, or enjoyment. We should avoid all innovations and all worldy influences in worship.

4. Those who deviate from His Word will be punished according to that Word.

5. All we have has come from God. We should be thankful, and should use what we have in ways that please Him.

6. There is need for a lively fear of God in our lives.

Let's Pray

Lord of Hosts,

You have chosen to make us a kingdom of royal priests

and a holy nation.

You have singled us out for Your Son,

made us Your own by His blood,

and granted us Your Holy Spirit.

Grant also that we live up to our duties before You,

and that we do so with all our heart

so that You will always be honored by us, as You ought to be honored.

In this way, we will be confident that You are guiding us toward the sure fulfillment of our holy hopes, and that we will at long last arrive at Your eternal kingdom.

May your Son, our Savior, rule us by His Spirit,

so that we will always be faithful to Him

and, in due time, share in the eternal glory

of our High Priest and the forerunner of our faith.

Amen.

SUBJECTS FOR DISCUSSION AND STUDY

- Compare similarities and differences between the roles of the priests and of Christian leaders in their various contexts.

- How does the worship of God shape our thinking about Him?

- Summarize what is said in Scripture about the way God is to be worshipped. Are there differences between worship in the temple and worship in the church? If there are, what are they and why do they exist?

- How can we cultivate caution in familial and congregational worship?

- Compare the characteristics of a faithful teacher of God's Word according to Malachi with what the New Testament has to say about the topic.

CHAPTER 4

Betrayals
(MALACHI 2:10–17)

Do we not all have one father? Did not one God create us? Why do we betray one another, to defile the covenant of our fathers? Judah has betrayed and an abomination has been done in Israel and in Jerusalem, because Judah has defiled the Lord's sanctity, which He loves, and taken the daughter of a foreign god for a wife. The LORD will cut off the person who will do this, [destroy] anyone awake or present to respond from the tents of Jacob and the presenter of offerings to the LORD of Hosts.

This also you do: you cover the altar of the LORD with tears, weeping and groaning, so that there is no more [room] to consider the offering—and I should be pleased with your peace offering? And you say, "For what reason?" Because the LORD has testified between you and the wife of your youth, whom you have betrayed though she is your friend and the woman of your covenant.

Did He not make them one? And has He not yet a remnant of spirit? And what does the one seek? A godly seed, that you keep watch over your spirits and that you do not betray the woman of your youth. "Because I hate divorce" says the Lord, the God of Israel, "and the covering of his cloak with violence," says the LORD of Hosts, "and you keep watch over your spirits and do not betray."

You have wearied the LORD with your words! And you say, "In what have we wearied [Him]?" In saying, "Whoever does evil is good in the sight of the Lord, and He delights in them" or, "where is the God of justice?"

This portion of the prophet's message is the most difficult in terms of its language. As a result, it needs to be carefully examined. The translation above does not make for good English (any more than Malachi's Hebrew meets modern standards of good Hebrew writing). It is intended to convey a clearer view of the difficulties to be found in the text than most translations allow. The reason for this is that translations tend to round the corners of the original in an effort to secure a more memorable, more literary rendering as well as clarify portions that would not otherwise be understood. Hopefully, the translation provided here will assist the reader of God's Word to grapple with the issues that Word raises.

There is more than one way to read what Malachi says in this passage. Commentators differ in their conclusions on the details but share an understanding of the general thrust. This passage is comprised of three subsections related to each other by a shared concern: unfaithfulness to covenants. Verses 10–12 speak of the covenantal unfaithfulness of the returnees in the context of society. God commanded the Israelites not to intermarry with the nations among whom they had settled. Israel was to be a distinct and separate people. Intermarriage was therefore a disavowal of the covenant. Verses 13–16 speak of disloyalty to the covenant of marriage. And verse 17 speaks of unfaithfulness to God and, by implication, to the covenant God made with Israel.

The portion as a whole is related to the one preceding in that they both deal with covenants and their transgression.

In the course of this passage, Malachi begins with gentle language, employing the first person plural (we). He moves on to speak more harshly, in the third person singular (Judah). He concludes with strong accusatory language, which employs the second person plural (you) and climaxes in the second person singular (you).

National Unfaithfulness

The first subsection relates to a trend among the returnees, including the priests, to wed non-Jewish wives. The background may be learned from the books of Ezra and Nehemiah. Contrary to what is commonly believed, the Law did not forbid intermarriage between Jews and Gentiles. On the contrary, a mixed multitude departed with the Israelites from Egypt and entered covenant at the foot of Mount Sinai. Tamar, Er's wife, Ruth the Moabitess, Rahab of Jericho, and Bathsheba (probably a

Hittite) are all examples of women from other nations who married into Israel.

What the Law forbade was marriage between Israel and the Canaanite nations that inhabited the country when Israel arrived to possess it:

> When the LORD your God brings you into the land you are entering to possess and drives out before you many nations—the Hittites, Girgashites, Amorites, Canaanites, Perizzites, Hivites and Jebusites, seven nations larger and stronger than you—and when the LORD your God has delivered them over to you and you have defeated them, then you must destroy them totally.

> Make no treaty with them, and show them no mercy. Do not intermarry with them. Do not give your daughters to their sons or take their daughters for your sons, for they will turn your children away from following Me to serve other gods, and the LORD's anger will burn against you and will quickly destroy you.

> This is what you are to do to them: Break down their altars, smash their sacred stones, cut down their Asherah poles, and burn their idols in the fire. For you are a people holy to the LORD your God. The LORD your God has chosen you out of all the peoples on the face of the earth to be His people, His treasured possession (Deuteronomy 7:1–6).

Ezra quoted this passage when he narrated his discussion with the leaders of the nation:

> The leaders came to me and said, "The people of Israel, including the priests and the Levites, have not kept themselves separate from the neighboring peoples with their detestable practices, like those of the Canaanites, Hittites, Perizzites, Jebusites, Ammonites, Moabites, Egyptians, and Amorites. They have taken some of their daughters as wives for themselves and their sons, and have mingled the holy race with the peoples around them. And the leaders and officials have led the way in this unfaithfulness" (Ezra 9:1–2).

A careful comparison with what is said in Deuteronomy (and in its parallel, Exodus 34:10–16) will show that the leaders in Ezra's day did not quote the Law exactly. They added the Egyptians to the list. However, in both cases, the emphasis is not on the list of nations but on the need to avoid intermarriage with those of the nations that inhabited the land lest they turn your children away from following Me to serve other gods. That is the main point, and that is the reason for the prohibition.

Ezra informs us of what, in fact, occurred in his day. Among the returnees, there were those who wedded women from the nations living in the land, Samaritans and Edomites, and some of the leaders and officials have led the way in this unfaithfulness. In response, Ezra publicly tore his clothes and began to mourn. Others, everyone who trembled at the words of the God of Israel, joined him.

Why? Not because they married foreign women. The reason was that the women they married were from the nations among whom they lived (note that phrase in what follows) and because these women were idol worshippers.

After a day of mourning, Ezra sought mercy from God (Ezra 9:6–15). Many of the people were affected by his actions (10:1). Among them was Shekaniah, son of Jehiel, who said to Ezra:

> We have been unfaithful to our God by marrying foreign women from the peoples around us. But in spite of this, there is still hope for Israel. Now let us make a covenant before our God to send away all these women and their children, in accordance with the counsel of my lord and of those who fear the commands of our God. Let it be done according to the Law. Rise up; this matter is in your hands. We will support you, so take courage and do it (**Ezra 10:2–4**).

Ezra responded by issuing, with the rest of the leadership, a dictum: Honor the LORD, the God of your ancestors, and do His will. Separate yourselves from the peoples around you and from your foreign wives (Ezra 10:11). The people responded by obeying.

Nehemiah reports that, during his first visit to Jerusalem, the people and their leaders:

> All who separated themselves from the neighboring peoples for the sake of the Law of God, together with their wives and all their sons and daughters who are able to understand, undertook an oath to now join their fellow Israelites the nobles, and bind themselves with a curse and an oath to follow the Law of God given through Moses the servant of God and to obey carefully all the commands, regulations, and decrees of the LORD our Lord. We promise not

to give our daughters in marriage to the peoples around us or take their daughters for our sons (**Nehemiah 10:28–30**).

This did not lead to a permanent resolution of the problem. When Nehemiah returned to Jerusalem for a second visit, he faced the same situation all over again. This time he resolved to handle it somewhat differently, by emphasizing intermarriage with women from any foreign nation. I saw men of Judah who had married women from Ashdod, Ammon, and Moab. Half of their children spoke the language of Ashdod or the language of one of the other peoples, and did not know how to speak the language of Judah (**Nehemiah 13:23–24**).

In response, Nehemiah tells us:

I rebuked them and called curses down on them. I beat some of the men and pulled out their hair. I made them take an oath in God's name and said: "You are not to give your daughters in marriage to their sons, nor are you to take their daughters in marriage for your sons or for yourselves. Was it not because of marriages like these that Solomon king of Israel sinned? Among the many nations there was no king like him. He was loved by his God, and God made him king over all Israel, but even he was led into sin by foreign women.

Must we hear now that you too are doing all this terrible wickedness and are being unfaithful to our God by marrying foreign women?" One of the sons of Joiada, son of Eliashib the high priest, was son-in-law to Sanballat the Horonite. And I drove him away from me. Remember them, my God, because they defiled the priestly office and the covenant of the priesthood and of the Levites. So I purified the priests and the Levites of everything foreign, and assigned them duties, each to his own task (**Nehemiah 13:25–30**).

This is the background to Malachi's rebuke. The importance of Israel's distinct national identity is at the heart of the prophet's words in this subsection. The returnees had broken the covenant God made with their forefathers and transgressed His commandments. They had done so because they lost hope for a national restoration. Losing that hope robbed them of motivation to maintain a national identity, to avoid intermingling with other nations, and to maintain their national religion.

That is exactly what is happening in Israel today. Many have lost hope in the fulfillment of Israel's national destiny. All that interests them is personal fulfillment, a respectable livelihood, a nice home, a periodic trip overseas, and a new car. The term "Jewish" has lost its value in their eyes. Some disavow the designation and prefer to describe themselves as Israelis. The history, customs, values, celebrations, and other symbols of national identity have little, if any, value in their eyes. They do not care if their children wed outside the nation or if the next generation loses its national identity.

Under the impact of a universalistic humanism, the nations of the west are likewise losing their national distinctiveness and merging into a hodge-podge of multiculturalism that is presumed to bring ultimate harmony. History, national customs, and values are thrown overboard, while a committed, determined minority threatens to engulf the spineless humanism that informs the rest.

Similarly, many in the church are no longer driven by the blessed hope. They do not long to be more godly, more holy, or to know, love, and serve God more. Their aspirations are summed up in a reasonable livelihood, a nice house, a periodic trip overseas, and a new car, and, oh yes, a raise from time to time. They are not driven by spiritual desires and have few, if any, moral aspirations. All that interests them has to do with this world.

For that reason, Christian truth, traditions, history, and customs do not stir their hearts. They are not concerned for the church, except as a social club. They are not engaged in serious Bible study or prayer. They do not mind forming intimate relations with non-Christians, they would gladly marry them (if they're good-looking), and their own Christian identity is not a matter of concern to them. They are too much like the world to be a Christian example, and their consciences are troubled only in the few good moments they might have.

National Cohesion and National Responsibility

Malachi appeals to the people of his generation on two bases— their obligations to God by covenant and creation: Do we not all have one father? Did not one God create us? Why do we betray one another, to defile the covenant of our fathers? Malachi is appealing to the people for the sake of their national cohesion. He stands alongside them and identifies himself with them—he addresses them as we. We have one Father. We are a nation created by the one God who exists (compare Isaiah 43:1). Now we betray one another. So too with mankind. We were all created by the one God who exists. Even as we struggle against the sins of our generation, we remain one with all mankind, united by a common father, a shared Creator, and a mutual responsibility. Mankind is one. Every man is under obligation toward his fellow man. All the more is this true of relations with our nation.

Israel was chosen for the sake of the nations. Jews betray their calling when they deny or neglect it, when they no longer believe that their national calling obliges them in the course of their everyday life.

We are brothers, says Malachi. We are brothers because we come from the one and selfsame father, meaning Abraham. We are one because the one and only God created us, for the sake of the family of nations, to be a distinct and separate nation as He entered into covenant with our forefathers at Mount Sinai. We are bound one to another. We are accountable to one another. We have no right to lead our lives as if the only valid considerations are how to successfully increase our income and secure our economic future.

Why do we betray one another? Our personal conduct has implications that exceed the private and the personal, and we must endeavor not to act in ways that affect others adversely. Selfish choices that do not take the will of God into account affect others in negative ways.

How can a Christian young man who is intimate with an unbeliever speak to her of the holiness of God? How can a Christian young woman in a relationship with an unbeliever teach him that God is to be loved above all others? How can an employer who does not treat his employees properly, or an employee who does not give his employer the best of his time and abilities, speak of the justice which God demands we show one another?

Our selfishness, compromise, immorality, pride, pursuit of pleasure and comfort, love for this world's trinkets—these all meaningfully impact others. Unbiblical behavior implies either that Christians are hypocrites or that the Gospel is not true. It certainly implies that God is less important than momentary satisfaction. What will our children learn from the way we live? What will our spouse deduce from our example? Why do we betray one another?

In addition to betraying each other, those of the returnees who broke covenant also betrayed God. That was the root of all their betrayals. How did they betray one other? By defiling the covenant of our fathers.

In what way did they transgress? Malachi replies: Judah has betrayed and an abomination has been done in Israel and in Jerusalem, because Judah has defiled the Lord's sanctity, which he loves, and taken the daughter of a foreign god for a wife.

Addressing the returnees as both Judah and Israel indicates that Malachi believed that small remnant of the people constituted the essence of the nation. That remnant was to inherit the promises made to the nation and therefore was obliged to fulfill the duties implied.

A foreign god is the god of a foreign nation. God was described above as the Creator of the Israelite nation. The daughter of a foreign god is, simply, a woman who worships a foreign god and who comes from a family who worships a foreign god.

Judah betrayed God, and the sons of Judah betrayed one another by wedding women who continued in their idolatry. This, says Malachi, is a betrayal and an abomination ... in Israel and in Jerusalem.

Forbidden Love

Why? Is every person not free to choose his or her spouse? No. We are not free to choose anything the LORD forbids. He forbids marriage and any other relationship that could cause us to deviate from His ways, just as He forbade the yoking-together of two different kinds of animals (Deuteronomy 22:10). Do not intermarry with them. Do not give your daughters to their sons or take their daughters for your sons, for they will turn your children away from following Me to serve other gods (Deuteronomy 7:1–6).

Paul referred to this in terms of the Christian life:

Do not be yoked together with unbelievers. For what do righteousness and wickedness have in common? Or what fellowship can light have with darkness? What harmony is there between Christ and Belial? Or what does a believer have in common with an unbeliever? What agreement is there between the temple of God and idols? For we are the temple of the living God. As God has said: "I will live with them and walk among them, and I will be their God, and they will be My people." Therefore, come out from them and be separate, says the Lord. "Touch no unclean thing, and I will receive you and I will be a Father to you, and you will be My sons and daughters, says the LORD Almighty" (2 Corinthians 6:14–18).

"But I love her" is not an excuse that God will accept. Some loves are forbidden. We often must forbid ourselves what our hearts long to have, just as we sometimes have to oblige ourselves with duties from which our heart longs to be free. Remember Nehemiah's words: Was it not because of marriages like these that Solomon king of Israel sinned? Among the many nations there was no king like him. He was loved by his God, and God made him king over all Israel, but even he was led into sin by foreign women.

Don't lie to yourself, "I'll bring her to Christ." Perhaps you will, but it is more likely that she will bring you to deny Christ. After all, your relationship with her is a step of denial. You are denying the authority of God's commandments and defiling His covenant by disobedience.

What will create the sudden turnaround and cause her to be influenced by your godliness, so well hidden in the push and shove of your relationship? You have sacrificed your faithfulness in order to maintain the relationship. Moral and spiritual compromise does not naturally incline to challenge unbelievers. It can teach them little of the holiness of God and of His right to be first in our lives. Such a relationship is nothing less than a breach of covenant with God and a breach of the covenant that binds you to fellow Christians. It is a defilement of God's name and a defilement of the holy people of God (compare Leviticus 19:8), whom He loves. That is why the choices made by the returnees in Malachi's day were more than personal choices. They had national ramifications.

Israel was to be a nation dedicated to God, and therefore distinct from the nations. Marriage with idolatrous women abrogated that distinctiveness and made Israel like any other nation. That is why Malachi says, The LORD will cut off the person who will do this, [destroy] anyone awake or to respond from the tents of Jacob and the presenter of offerings to the LORD of Hosts.

To be cut off was the ultimate punishment. Even when cutting off implied execution, the main part of the punishment was not death. It was removal from the people and therefore from the covenant promises. Those who wed idolatrous women transgressed the covenant in a fundamental way. According to the covenant (Exodus 12:15, 19; 31:14; Leviticus 7:20; 14:4; 20:5–6; and many others), they are to be cut off.

Israel was commanded to remove from the nation all who transgressed God's commandments in such a way. Here it is God who does the cutting, and it is carried out to the extreme end. No one from the tents of Jacob is left awake or present to respond. This expression is found in the Bible only here. There is a similar Arabic expression that may well explain the Hebrew: the one awake is the guard who watches over the camp at night. The one present to respond is the guard's replacement. He must identify himself by responding to the guard's challenge with an agreed sign. These two would be the only individuals awake in the camp, so the expression means, "down to the last." The presenter of offerings is an individual who brings offerings to the LORD in His temple.

The LORD will cut off the person who will do this, [destroy] anyone awake or to respond from the tents of Jacob and the presenter of offerings to the LORD of Hosts. That is to say, he who sins by taking a foreign wife may belong to the tents of Jacob, but the LORD will remove him and any like him, from the nation, down to the last person. No one will be left, not even to bring offerings to the LORD because even the priests will be cut off. It is difficult to imagine a more terrible catastrophe than to leave the nation without priests to lead the worship of God and teach the people His ways.

Hypocrisy in the Worship of God

As if it were not enough that the people intermarried with idolatresses, Malachi says, This also you do: you cover the altar of the LORD with tears, weeping and groaning, so that there is no more [room] to consider the offering—and I should be pleased with your peace offering?

In addition to intermarriage, This also you do. What else did the priests do? You cover the altar of the LORD with tears, weeping and groaning, so that there is no more [room] to consider the offering. At the same time that you sin against the LORD and against each other, you cover the altar with your weeping and praying. The priests were religious but not moral—and I should be pleased with your peace offering? The LORD asks.

The priests had lost all sense of shame. Their consciences seemed to have been seared with a hot iron. They were no longer sensitive to their guilt. That is what sin does. Promising us life, it robs us of the essence of a happy life—an alert yet clean conscience. Their consciences had been defiled and, as a result, lost the ability to trouble. "I feel at peace with what I am doing" does not mean a thing. It cannot be a moral guide. An uninformed, desensitized conscience will inevitably mislead us.

Obviously, the priests' tears and prayers were not expressions of sorrow over sin. They were not tears and prayers of repentance. The priests wept over the loss of their earthly pleasure, over the pain of punishment in the loss of crops, and the straitened political circumstances. There was no indication of a real desire to follow after the Lord. How could they think the LORD would take positive note of such religiosity?! Malachi appeals to their reason, asking in the name of the Lord: I should be pleased with your peace offering?

Marriage

The priests' reason was skewed. Hearing Malachi, they dared to ask: For what reason? Why will God not accept our ritual, our earnest prayers, and our offerings? Is it not enough that we do what we do? No, says Malachi. It is not. Empty ritual is just that: empty. It has no substance and leads nowhere. It certainly does not persuade God.

You are missing the main point of the Law, which is holiness in the fear of God, a sincere concern for others, and an honest loyalty to the terms of the covenant. As someone put it many years later, religion that God our Father accepts as pure and faultless is this: to look after orphans and widows in their distress and to keep oneself from being polluted by the world (James 1:27).

Do you want to know why God rejects your prayers and your offerings? I'll tell you: Because the LORD has testified between you and the wife of your youth, whom you have betrayed though she is your friend and the woman of your covenant. Did He not make them one? And has He not yet a remnant of spirit? And what does the one seek? A godly seed, that you keep watch over your spirits and that you do not betray the woman of your youth. "Because I hate divorce," says the Lord, the God of Israel, "and the covering of his cloak with violence," says the LORD of Hosts, "and you keep watch over your spirits and do not betray."

Apparently, not only did the returnees, priests included, wed idolatrous women, but they divorced their previous wives to do so. God views such a breach of the marriage covenant as breach of covenant with Him. Although polygamy—the taking of more than one wife—was still permitted in Israel,[3] the majority preferred monogamy. Usually, only the rich

---

[3] There is evidence that polygamy was permitted in Israel until the second or even third century. Josephus Flavius, the Jewish historian who lived in the first century, states that Judaism permitted more than one wife. Justin Martyr lived a short time later. The fact that Rabbi Gershom (the eleventh century) had to legislate against the practice shows that it was still common.

could afford the luxury of multiple wives. Consequently, if one of the returnees fancied another woman, the only way he could afford her would be to divorce his wife.

Malachi does not rebuke the priests because they preferred foreign women to their Jewish wives. There is not even a hint of nationalism in his complaint. To the contrary, he later defends foreigners living among the people (3:5). The prohibition outlawing the wedding of foreign women was not a form of racism but a way to preserve Israel's loyalty to God. Malachi rebukes the priests for weakening the institution of marriage, regardless of whether their wives were Jewish or Gentile. In so doing, he affords us an important lesson on the way Scripture views this important institution.

First, Malachi determines that God is the guardian and the protector of the marriage covenant. Marriage is not a secular act, an agreement between two sides interested in a relationship. Marriage is an act of religious significance, even when the partners do not intend for it to be so. God is involved in every marriage, and He Himself testifies against those who break covenant: The LORD has testified between you and the wife of your youth. Marriage is meant to reflect something of the life of God. A man and a woman, two who are distinct one from another, become one. Just as there is a unity and a distinction within the godhead; there are three who are one.

Second, Malachi determines that a breach of the marriage covenant is an act of betrayal. The LORD has testified between you and the wife of your youth, whom you have betrayed. Just as the priests and the people betrayed God, so too did they betray their wives.

The God who made the people into one nation had also united men and women in their marriage relationship. The prophet assumes that there is a logical and moral analogy between the unity of the nation and the unity of the family, between the covenant God made with Israel and the covenant between a man and his wife. Just as the national covenant with God ought not to be breached, so it should be with the marriage covenant.

Malachi's designation of a wife is reminiscent of Proverb's description of the woman, who has left the partner of her youth and ignored the covenant she made before God (Proverbs 2:17). Incidentally, such a view runs completely contrary to the chauvinistic assumptions that were at the root of many marriages and of the attitude of many societies toward women. Without denying the differences of role, capacity, and propensity between men and women, it views them as equal in value.

Third, Malachi describes the relationship between marriage partners in particularly warm terms. The woman is described as the wife of your youth ... your friend. Malachi does not subscribe to the modern view in which a woman passes from one man to another until she finds Mr. Wonderful. Malachi has no room for trial experiences. When she was young, in the height of her beauty, he says, your wife left her father's home and commenced a shared life with you. She became your friend, a partner to your struggles, disappointments, efforts, and successes. She gave birth to your children and managed the affairs of your home. When you were sad, she gave you comfort. When you encountered difficulties, she encouraged you. When you were happy, she was the first to share your joy. Calvin says in this regard and on this verse, "We see that, when a husband and his wife live together for many years, their love for one another blossoms to a very old age because their hearts were united when they were young."[4]

Scripture paints a delightful picture of marriage and of familial relations: loyalty and friendship, intimacy and mutuality, kindness and appreciation, giving and receiving that stand the test of time and are not jaded by circumstances or years. In a proper marriage, husband and wife are friends, true and full partners in the adventure that is life. They have no secrets. They act with complete transparency toward each other. They are forever laughing together, working together, playing and crying together, building together, and celebrating with one heart the life that God gave them. He consults her, and she consults him. He teaches her, and she teaches him.

Marriage is meant to provide the husband with a helper suited to him (Genesis 2:18). The Hebrew actually speaks of a helper over against him, that is to say, compatible with him in the sense that she has what he does not and lacks what he has so that they complement each other by their differences. Marriage is meant to provide the wife with a lover, a caregiver, a protector, and a leader. It is meant to provide the husband with a friend, a loving critic, a supporter, and a confidant. A man's wife brings to the relationship abilities, propensities, and a viewpoint he does not have. He provides her with similar complementary contributions.

Marriage is a sanctifying, edifying friendship and a sharing of hearts, mutual support, mutual consideration, and uncompromising loyalties.

---

[4] John Calvin, *Calvin's Commentaries* (reprint, Grand Rapids, MI: Baker Books, 2003), 15:553.

There is no more wonderful, more constructive a relationship than marriage when conducted by the will and commandments of God. No institution can bring greater happiness. Now that she has aged, her breasts have fallen, her skin wrinkled, and her stomach swelled, don't cast her aside as if she were a used rag.

We have made earlier references to the fourth point, but it is time to spell it out: The marital relationship is described as a covenant. She is ... the woman of your covenant. In the ancient world, as in our day, marriage was generally viewed as a contract between two adults (today) or two families (in ancient days). Marriage took the form of a covenant only when it had political implications, as when the partners were the children of warring families or of different nations.

Scripture, on the other hand, considers all marriages to be a covenant. A covenant is not a temporary, utilitarian arrangement. It is a solemn undertaking—a lifelong undertaking that is valid for as long as both of the partners are alive, for good or for ill, in sickness and in health, come what may. Covenants were established in the presence of God, who witnessed the mutual undertakings of the partners.

One could exit a contract by completing its terms. These were often quite burdensome because they were meant to reduce the likelihood of either of the partners exiting the agreement. But there was no moral turpitude in doing so as long as the terms were met. Not so with a covenant. Covenants had no terminus. All breaches of covenant were considered immoral.

If someone is not true to his covenant partner, can he or she be trusted to be true to anyone else? If someone is capable of lying to the person closest to him, to his life-partner, his friend, and his woman of covenant, he is capable of lying to anyone. Honesty is of one substance. An individual who shows himself unreliable in one sphere is not to be trusted in others. A person who is capable of betraying the woman of his youth will betray anyone, any cause, any charge, and any trust.

Covenant, then, means a serious commitment. Its breach is a terrible thing—treason, not less. God, who witnessed the establishment of the covenant, is also its guardian. His presence and His commands render the relationship a covenant. Whoever breaches covenant will have to answer to God Himself, and when God testifies against someone (the LORD has testified between you and the wife of your youth), none is left to defend him.

Fifth, Malachi invites us back to the very beginnings of history before sin entered the world so that we will understand that marriage, the covenant between man and woman, belongs to the foundations of human existence. It was a gift of God when the man and his woman still had access to the Garden of Eden.

Did He not make them one? That is to say, did God not make the two to be one? Malachi is referring to Genesis 2:24: "A man leaves his father and mother and is united to his wife, and they become one flesh." Malachi is reminding the hearers of the essence of marriage. The two are no longer two apart but two who have been united by the commandment of God into one. The covenant of marriage has altered the nature of the relations between the man and the woman. A new kind of relationship has been established, one that can only exist within the context of a covenantal marriage. They become one. That is the meaning of the titles Malachi has employed to describe the wife: the woman of your youth … your friend and the woman of your covenant.

Some understand the question which I have translated, did He not make them one, as a repetition of Malachi's earlier question, did not one make them, the one who made them being God. It is possible to translate the Hebrew in that way, but it seems to me that the context requires the translation I have preferred, and that Malachi is referring to two different events. Of course, it is for you, dear reader, to decide how you read this portion of God's Word.

And has He not yet a remnant of spirit. The meanings attached to this statement are as numerous as those who choose to comment on them. Ancient commentators are equally divided. Obviously, Malachi's words should be understood in context. The context relates to marriage and to national cohesion. The term He apparently refers to God, who made man and woman one. It seems likely, therefore, that what Malachi is saying is that God is capable of doing more than making the two to be one. Perhaps he is saying that, had God wished it, He could have made three or four into one—in other words, that he is speaking in defense of monogamy.

This is unlikely. Malachi was addressing the people because they allowed themselves to divorce their wives and wed idol worshippers, not because they took additional wives. So far as I am concerned, this statement remains an enigma. Hopefully, God will yet shed light on this portion of His Word.

And what does the one seek? A godly seed. Malachi continues with his string of questions, all geared to remind his hearers of important truths. The one seeking are the husband and wife after they have been united (Did he not make them one). What are they to seek? A godly seed. They are to seek children dedicated to God (see Ezra 9:2), the fruit of a marriage blessed by Him and conducted in accordance with His commandments, children who are brought up in the ways of God rather than in those dictated by idolatry. Such a seed is unlikely when brought up in a house divided against itself, in which the husband worships the Lord and the mother worships idols. The children would, at best, be confused, exposed to idolatrous influences, and liable to idolatrous practices.

Malachi expects his hearers to prefer God's will to theirs and God's commandments to other considerations. He expects them to control their desires and to deny themselves so that their marriages would accord to His commandments, not to the dictates of their hearts. He expects them to be persistent in loyalty toward their spouses, not to go captive after other women. He expects them to prefer true, lifelong love to the rush of excitement that can be obtained by betrayal. He therefore says, keep watch over your spirits and that you do not betray the woman of your youth. Do not betray one another (v. 10), and do not betray the woman of your youth.

Let's think for a moment about these words. Malachi has described the wives of the Israelites as the woman of your youth, the one and only, she who loved you from your youth, who was faithful to you all these years, and you to her. He chose to use this designation to emphasize the grievousness of betrayal and to stir in the hearts of the people memories of the sweet, clean love they enjoyed in the past. He sought to awaken their consciences. Next, he states that the way to avoid betrayal is to keep watch over your spirits.

How does one keep watch? By avoiding intimacy of any kind with another woman; by distancing oneself from temptations and from circumstances that might become an opportunity for temptation; by cultivating intimacy, affection, and friendship with the woman of our youth, and with none other.

Marriages are to be worked at. They don't just happen to be successful. They need to be cultivated, watched over, and defended. Families that fail to create emotional intimacy are headed for disaster. Emotionally starved men and women are exposed to temptation from those who will take advantage of their hunger and promise—even by way of an unintended hint—to satisfy that hunger for the price of betrayal.

Husbands and wives need to teach and to learn from each other how to cultivate, express, and deepen intimacy. Marriages need to be fortified by a deeply felt comprehension of the significance of the marriage covenant and of the way Scripture views marriage. That is exactly what Malachi is teaching us here and in what he has to say next.

Divorce

Keep watch over your spirits ... do not betray the woman of your youth means, control yourselves. Direct your wishes by the Word of God. Why should the returnees do this? If there was no other reason to motivate them to faithfulness, Malachi offers an important reason: "Because I hate divorce," says the Lord, the God of Israel, "and the covering of his cloak with violence," says the LORD of Hosts.

Malachi attributes two titles to God: Lord, the God of Israel and the LORD of Hosts. The first is meant to remind the people that God is the God of the covenant. He remains such even when Israel sins. Israel should therefore fear Him and return to His commandments. He is no strange God to Israel. He is the God of your covenant. You are obliged to be true to Him. The second title brings to mind His holy terror and the greatness of His power. God rules all the hosts, all powers that exist.

I hate divorce does not need to be explained, although we would do well to remember the vehemence with which that statement is made.

Some ancient translations render these words in direct contrast to their intent, as if the prophet said "if you hate [her]—divorce [her]" (the first person pronoun, "I," is not in the text. It is, however, strongly implied). The implication is that Malachi was legitimatizing divorce. Certain well-known rabbinic dictums state, "even if she burnt his soup," divorce is permitted.

Not so. God hates divorce. He hates betrayal, and divorce is a major kind of betrayal. It is not a legitimate option.[5] There are very few things

---

[5] While other portions of Scripture very slightly modify this absolute statement, our study is of Malachi, not of the general, but highly important, subject of marriage and divorce. We must, therefore, limit ourselves to what Malachi says. Suffice it to say that every other statement of Scripture regarding marriage and divorce is based on the foundation laid here. Divorce is never permitted except where the marriage covenant has already been breached in a radical, fundamental way.

the Scriptures describe as hateful to God. Divorce is one. God is not indifferent to divorce and certainly does not condone it. He hates it.

The returnees could have protested, with good reason, "But Moses permitted a man to write his wife a certificate of divorce and send her away! (Deuteronomy 24:1–4). How can you say that God hates what He permitted?" The answer is ready. God indeed hates what He permitted. Permission was granted at the time for reasons we need not go into here because they will not help us understand Malachi's message. We do not pit one Scripture against another but instead find the truth in the tensions created by what appears to be conflicting statements. It is enough for us to recognize that Malachi's words are as much the Word of God as are those which permitted divorce. It is also enough for us to take into account that God moved Malachi to describe divorce in terms of betrayal. After all, from the beginning, He made the two into one and ordered that their oneness should be so fundamental that it alters and supersedes all previous relationships.

Malachi next describes divorce as a form of violence. The Hebrew term (*hamas*) speaks of the use of violence to take something that does not belong to us. So, for example, Sarah complains to Abraham after he took her maidservant, Hagar, You are responsible for the wrong I am suffering (Genesis 16:5).The words the wrong I am suffering are one word in Hebrew: *hamas*.

God is said here to hate two things: divorce and the covering of violence. These two are one. The cloak of a person who divorces his wife cannot hide the violence of his deed, however much he might try to hide it. Divorce is a form of violence. However amicable it may sometimes seem to be, it remains a violent act, for two who have become one can separate only if torn apart. The cloak (outer garment) of whoever engaged in such an act is covered with indications of violence for all to see and recognize him for what he is. In other words, it cannot be hidden.

This is what the Bible calls sin with a high hand—premeditated, arrogant sin. As Calvin puts it, in this connection "Your hypocrisy is great. Were there any fear of God in you, you would have been faithful one to another in marriage."

Whoever wants to excuse his action by the permission Moses granted is free to do so. But he exposes himself to the terrible anger of God because such a person has chosen to betray the woman with whom he is in covenant. He will give account to God for that choice. The wise will not make light of these severe words from Malachi; if nothing else, their fear will preserve them from an irredeemable catastrophe. That is why the prophet ends by saying keep watch over your spirits and do not betray.

Here, spirit is a euphemism for desire, a hunger for something (see Proverbs 16:32, where "self-control" is, in Hebrew, "control of one's spirit"). Don't follow your spirits. Don't follow your hearts. Don't think that as long as you believe that what you want is permitted and your conscience does not trouble you, you're at liberty to do what you please. Don't think that if your heart prompts you to do something, it is necessarily the right thing to do. Keep watch over your spirits. Control your heart; don't let it control you. Today's pleasure may lead to eternal suffering.

Malachi ends this section of his message with words of general rebuke which are directly related to what he said so far: You have wearied the LORD with your words! And you say, "In what have we wearied [Him]?" In saying, "whoever does evil is good in the sight of the Lord, and He delights in them," or, "where is the God of justice?"

In spite of the people's many efforts, blessing was not forthcoming. The people had exerted much effort in returning to the land and resettling it. They had labored hard at reconstructing the temple, restoring the city, and repairing its walls. They had been given great hopes regarding the success of their efforts. But the Edomites and the Samaritans were as strong as ever and the returnees almost as weak as when they first arrived. So they asked, Where is the God of justice? Where is the justice He promised to establish in the world? Are we not God's people? Why does He bless our enemies and bypass us?

This was a typical case of blame-shifting. Unwilling to examine themselves, they sought to lay the blame for their situation on God. They were more willing to describe Him as unjust than to admit their own guilt!

God replies, "You are overturning the order of things, and I am weary of such behavior. You are not seeking Me, nor are you seeking to understand My ways. You transgress My Law and expect Me to bless you, simply because I covenanted to do so. But you conveniently forget your side of the covenant. You expect Me to keep covenant even when you do not. Your question is a complaint, a denial of My justice, as if you deserved to be blessed by virtue of the very covenant which you have not kept.

"You charge the judge of all the earth with doing wrong. You dare say, 'Whoever does evil is good in the sight of the Lord, and He delights in them.' By such thoughts you speak of Me as if I love evil and am pleased when evil is done, as if I am unjust in not blessing you."

LET'S SUMMARIZE

1. God created the people of Israel and gave them a national calling. They should be true to that calling—and we to ours—in the teeth of any difficulties that threaten to divert our attention or drive us to despair.

2. Despair is not an option so long as God rules the world. We, and Israel, should trust, and our trust should lead to obedience.

3. Israel should retain its distinct identity, and so should we Christians. We should not merge into our surroundings but dare to be different. Among other things, this means we are not to wed those who do not share our love and fear of the Lord.

4. Marriage is dear in the eyes of the LORD and a source of blessing to mankind. The relations between a husband and wife are meant for deep friendships, mutual affection, and uncompromising loyalty. These we should cultivate meticulously and guard carefully.

5. Any breach of the covenant of marriage is hateful to God. To divorce is to break covenant with God, with those around us, and with our spouses.

LET'S PRAY

Lord of Hosts,

we are inclined to evil of every kind

and daily transgress Your covenant of grace with us.

Do not deal with us as we deserve.

Teach us to guide our wills by Your Word,

to be faithful to the covenant of our marriage,

and to control our bodily and emotional desires.

Strengthen us by Your Spirit

so that we are faithful to our fellows

and to the members of our families,

that we cherish the unity of the Spirit,

and stubbornly maintain that unity.

In spite of the many efforts of the tempter

to distance us from You and from Your ways,

may it please you that we will continue

in obedience to Your Word

and in pure confidence in our calling and election,

by which You have received us

through the merits of Your only Son, our Savior.

May it please You to enable us to persist in faith until the end,

and that we at long last will be brought

into Your eternal kingdom

through the merits of Jesus' perfect sacrifice.

Amen.

SUBJECTS FOR DISCUSSION AND STUDY

- How valid is the call for Jewish Christians to retain their national identity today?

- If it is valid, how may they do so without disaffecting the unity of the church or the principle of equality among believers?

- How should Christians retain their distinct identity in a non-Christian environment?

- What can we learn about the proper use of Scripture from the way Ezra and Nehemiah used the Law?

- What steps ought we to take to strengthen our marriages?

CHAPTER 5

The Refiner's Fire
(MALACHI 3:1–18)

This chapter divides naturally into three sections (four in Hebrew; vv. 19–24 in English are the end of chapter three of the Hebrew Old Testament, and there is not another chapter). The three sections are verses 1–4, 5–12, and 13–18. This chapter and the next are in the first person singular, with God addressing the people directly.

Chapter Three continues in the style of the first two chapters, in the form of a dialogue between God and the people, primarily through accusatory questions from God, evasive responses from the priest or the people, and a response from God which normally includes a warning, a threat or—surprisingly—a promise.

Some prefer to link the closing verse of the previous chapter with the beginning of this chapter. That verse serves as an excellent summary of what was said in chapter two, which is apparently why the Masorites,[6] who divided the Hebrew Bible into chapters and verses, preferred to link it as they did. This verse can also serve as an excellent introduction to what is about to be said. In the long run, 2:17 links the topics discussed in chapters two and three. It is worth remembering that the chapter and verse division is not inspired and that there is room for differences.

---

[6] The term *Masorites* comes from a Hebrew word (*masor*) that means *to be handed down*, and ultimately came to mean *tradition* (*masoret*). The Masorites were Jewish scholars (most of who belonged to the Karaite sect of Judaism) who, between the seventh and the eleventh centuries, determined the Hebrew text of the Old Testament and added its vowels (the Bible was originally written with consonants and without vowels as Hebrew is written today). The chapter and verse division came still later, sometime in the fifteenth century.

Another important link between this chapter and the one preceding is the question, Where is the God of justice? God answers that question in the chapter before us: I will draw near to you in justice.

"I am sending My messenger and he will clear the way before Me, and suddenly will the Lord you are seeking come to His temple, and the angel of the covenant whom you desire, behold he comes," says the LORD of Hosts.

"And who can cope with the Day of His Coming? And who shall be able to stand when He is revealed? Because He is like a refiner's fire and like launderer's soap, and He will sit like a refiner and a purifier of silver, and He will purge the sons of Levi, and He will purge them like gold and like silver [are purged of their dross], and they will become those who bring offerings to the LORD in righteousness. And the offering of Judah and of Jerusalem will be pleasing to the LORD as in the distant past and in former years.

"And I will draw near to you in judgment, and I will be a witness quick to testify against the magicians and the adulterers and those who swear falsehoods and who suppress the wages of hired workers, the widow and the orphan and the stranger they turn away [from justice], and do not fear Me", says the LORD of Hosts.

"Because I am the Lord, I do not change and you, sons of Jacob, are not destroyed. From the days of your forefathers you have departed from My ways and not kept [them]. Return to Me and I will return to you," says the LORD of Hosts.

"And you said, 'in what shall we return?' Will a man rob God? But you have robbed Me. And you say, 'In what have we robbed You?' In the tithe and in the goodwill offering. You are cursed with a curse. It is Me that the whole nation is robbing. Bring all of the tithe to the storehouse and there will be food in My house, and try Me in this," says the LORD of Hosts, "if I will not open the floodgates of heaven and pour out on you a blessing that has no end, and I will rebuke the devourer, and he will not destroy the fruit of your land and the vine will not be fruitless in the field. And all the nations will consider you happy, because you will be a desirable land," says the LORD of Hosts.

"Your words against Me are strong," says the Lord. "And you said, 'what have we said about You?' You said, 'It is to no purpose to serve the Lord' and 'what profit [is there in that] we have remained true to Him and conducted ourselves as mourners before the LORD of Hosts? But now we consider the arrogant to be happy, and evil-doers prosper, they put God to the test and escaped.'"

Then those who feared the LORD spoke one to another, and the LORD listened and heard and wrote a book of remembrance [to be kept] before Him about those who feared the LORD and thought on His name. "And they will be mine," says the LORD of Hosts, "for the Day when I make them a special possession, and I will have mercy on them like a man has mercy on his son who serves him, and you will again see the difference between a righteous and an evil man, between one who serves God and one who does not" (Malachi 3:1–18).

As a background to this chapter, we shall summarize the message of the previous chapters:

In Malachi 1:1–5, God showed His love for Israel in the way He preferred Jacob to Esau (Esau is Edom, Israel's active foe at the time).[7] Evidence of God's love for Israel and hatred of Esau was to be found in the finality of the desolation that reigned in the land of Edom in contrast to Israel's restoration. Every effort on Edom's part to rebuild the land would end in failure. On the other hand, Israel's return to the land was yet to be successful, if only the people remained faithful. They would witness this difference between their fate and that of the nations and, in response, praise the Lord, who rules over nations (not just over Israel).

In Malachi 1:6–14, God is not receiving from Israel the honor He deserves. Instead, the people bring Him faulty offerings. It would be better if they did not worship at all than that they worship as they do, for God is great and His honor is great. Even among the nations, there are those who offer Him better worship than that offered by the priests to the tem-

---

[7] We do not have space to survey the history of ongoing animosity between the two nations. It is important, however, to note that the Edomites had spread over large tracts of Judah during the seventy years of Judah's exile in Babylon, and that the return of Judeans to the land provoked a struggle between the two nations.

ple in Jerusalem. Such worship dishonors the Lord. Whoever treats the honor of God in such a way is cursed.

Malachi 2:1-9. If the priests do not alter their behavior, God will punish them according to the covenant. They will learn from this that Malachi is indeed a messenger of the Lord, sent for the defense of the covenant God made with Levi to bring them to serve Him faithfully.

This covenant promised the priests life and peace on condition that they follow in the footsteps of those of their forefathers who feared the LORD and taught the truth of the Law, whose faithfulness motivated many to forsake their sins. That is the priest's role, for he is a messenger of the LORD of Hosts. The priests of Malachi's day had departed from the path and transgressed the covenant. They are therefore not honored by the people, nor should they be honored.

Malachi 2:10-17. Not only the priests are guilty of betrayal; the people have also been unfaithful, betraying the covenant God made with their forefathers by betraying the covenants of marriage in divorcing their wives and wedding idolatrous women. God made Adam and Eve to be one, and He expects husbands and wives to bring a holy, God-fearing progeny. He made the people one, and the people should maintain that national cohesiveness. God hates divorce. The people should therefore keep watch over their spirit and not betray one another.

The people are wearisome to God because they are turning the order of the world on its head, describing evil as good and complaining to God as if He is uninvolved in what happens to them.

The Priests' Moral Transformation

I am sending My messenger and he will clear the way before Me. It is impossible to read these words without recognizing the parallels in Exodus 23:20-25 and Isaiah 40:1-11, especially in light of the historical context of these portions of the Scriptures. In Exodus 23, God says:

See, I am sending an angel ahead of you to guard you along the way and to bring you to the place I have prepared. Pay attention to him and listen to what he says. Do not rebel against him; he will not forgive your rebellion, since My Name is in him.

If you listen carefully to what he says and do all that I say, I will be an enemy to your enemies and will oppose those who oppose you. My angel will go ahead of you and bring you into the

land of the Amorites, Hittites, Perizzites, Canaanites, Hivites, and
Jebusites, and I will wipe them out. Do not bow down before their
gods or worship them or follow their practices. You must demolish them and break their sacred stones to pieces.

Worship the LORD your God and His blessing will be on your
food and water. I will take away sickness from among you.

The words, I am sending an angel ahead of you, are reflected in Malachi's, I am sending My messenger. We can probably assume that Malachi
was hinting at a new exodus that the messenger of the LORD will ac-
complish, a motif which served repeatedly in the Old Testament to speak
of a great work of salvation (Isaiah 40–55 is but one obvious example.
Every biblical promise of a return to the land and many promised acts of
redemption are couched in terms reminiscent of the Exodus).

There are great similarities between the two passages:

1. Malachi's wording does not allow for a distinction to be drawn between the Lord and His messenger. That is also true of the statement quoted above from Exodus. The name of the LORD is "in"
   the messenger, who will not bear with the sins of the people, that
   is to say, he will not forgive them. Forgiving and not forgiving is an
   act which the Hebrew Bible reserves for God Himself. This is a hint
   of the divine nature of the messenger. Not only so, but when the
   messenger speaks, it is God who is speaking.

   So too in the passage from Malachi. Some English translations
   tend to obscure the fact that the Hebrew does not clearly indicate
   if the messenger God will send is the "Lord" who is to come or the
   angel of the covenant, who will sit to judge and purge the priests
   and people (acts ascribed in the Bible to God). In other words, it
   is not quite clear whether the messenger is or is not the LORD of
   Hosts Himself.

2. God, Moses is told, will protect His people through the messenger
   who will go before them and bring them to the land although others then resided in Canaan. Idolatry is not to be practiced. Faithfulness will be rewarded: Worship the LORD your God, and His blessing will be on your food and water. I will take away sickness from

among you. By implication, if the people are not faithful, they will experience plague and hunger.

According to Malachi, it is the Lord's messenger who will come to punish the sinners and bring the people to where the LORD would have them, but the goal is no longer the land of Canaan. The land has receded, and the goal is now distinctly spiritual and moral: He will purge the sons of Levi, and He will purge them like gold and like silver [are purged of their dross], and they will become those who bring offerings to the LORD in righteousness.

This is a hint, and more than a hint, of a spiritual exodus and a spiritual inheritance. Like other Old Testament prophets, Malachi takes up the theme of the historical exodus from Egypt, heightens it, and then uses it to describe an eschatological redemption that will constitute a perfect priesthood and a perfect people, both engaged in perfect worship.

Although we must not lose sight of the fact that this inheritance is described in terms of the temple ritual, we ought not to ignore the indications that Malachi is thinking in terms that far exceed that ritual, as the exodus he perceives exceeds the departure from Egypt.

Much like Mark, in chapter 1:1–3, Malachi conflates the passage from Exodus with a distinctly messianic passage from Isaiah 40:

Comfort, comfort My people, says your God. Speak tenderly to Jerusalem, and proclaim to her that her hard service has been completed, that her sin has been paid for; that she has received from the LORD's hand double for all her sins.

A voice of one calling: "In the wilderness prepare the way for the LORD; make straight in the desert a highway for our God. Every valley shall be raised up, every mountain and hill made low; the rough ground shall become level, the rugged places a plain. And the glory of the LORD will be revealed, and all people will see it together. For the mouth of the LORD has spoken."

A voice says, "Cry out." And I said, "What shall I cry?" "All people are like grass, and all their faithfulness is like the flowers

of the field. The grass withers and the flowers fall, because the
breath of the LORD blows on them. Surely the people are grass.
The grass withers and the flowers fall, but the Word of our God
endures forever."

You who bring good news to Zion, go up on a high mountain.
You who bring good news to Jerusalem, lift up your voice with a
shout, lift it up, do not be afraid; say to the towns of Judah, "Here
is your God!" See, the Sovereign LORD comes with power, and He
rules with a mighty arm. See, His reward is with Him, and His rec-
ompense accompanies Him. He tends His flock like a shepherd:
He gathers the lambs in His arms and carries them close to His
heart; He gently leads those that have young (vv. 1–11).

According to Isaiah, the people were in exile due to their sin. Their
spirits were low as were the spirits of the returnees in Malachi's day. Isaiah's words were meant to encourage the people and, in this way, prepare
the way of the Lord. This last phrase is taken up by Malachi, who says in
the name of the LORD that the messenger of the LORD will come, and
he will clear the way before Me. The messenger of the LORD is about to
come to bless the people by preparing them for the LORD Himself. Israel
is, indeed, weak like weightless chaff that every wind can blow away. But
the LORD will come in His mighty strength and remove every obstacle.
No mountain and no valley will be permitted to block Him as He makes
His way to bless His people. No difficulty will stop Him.

Some read the Hebrew הנני, translated by the NIV as I will send, as if
the reference is to an event to take place in Malachi's immediate future
("I am sending"). Others insist that the reference is to a more distant
event. Our task is to understand the Scriptures, not to make them fit a
predetermined frame of reference. We must therefore examine this word
regardless of frameworks that have taken shape in the course of our previous study of Scripture. Only then may we examine that framework in
the light of our findings and seek to relate the two.

Of course, Scripture texts are to be understood in context, including the wider context of the whole Word of God. We do not expect one
Scripture to contradict another (although as we have seen, this sometimes *seems* to be the case). Encountering a word or a passage that can be
read in more than one way, we ought to opt for the most natural, most
immediate possibility in the historical and linguistic context in which the
passage is found.

Obviously, Malachi's message could only have meaning to his generation if it had reference to that generation. Fulfillment could be immediate or distant, but there had to be an immediate reference to the time the message was spoken. After all, Malachi was not giving the people an abstract of future developments. He intended his hearers to draw conclusions for their own time and circumstances. However we understand the passage, we must ensure that our understanding leaves ample room for practical application to Malachi's original audience.

Scripture indeed teaches that the future has implications for the present and the future. But this cannot always determine the meaning of a word. Nor can the Hebrew word הנני determine whether or not Malachi is speaking of a proximate or a distant future. Unless there are clear indications otherwise, texts should first be assumed to relate to their immediate historical and linguistic context. Future reference should be attributed only to what cannot be attributed to the period contemporary with or immediately following the days of the prophet. That is what we endeavor to do in what follows.

It is quite possible that Malachi's language does not refer to chronology (an immediate or a more distant fulfillment) but to the suddenness of the messenger's appearance, who will suddenly appear, to be followed with equal suddenness by the Lord Himself. If that is how Malachi should be read. The prophet is encouraging his despairing hearers to motivate them to reassume their national duties. A sudden divine intervention is to be expected at any time. Since there is no indication of timing, the people should be up and doing, ready for His coming.

The messenger will come to prepare the way for the Lord, just as a herald went in those days ahead to announce and prepare the way for the king. As Isaiah put it: A voice of one calling: "In the wilderness prepare the way for the LORD; make straight in the desert a highway for our God. Every valley shall be raised up, every mountain and hill made low; the rough ground shall become level, the rugged places a plain. And the glory of the LORD will be revealed, and all people will see it together. For the mouth of the LORD has spoken." (Isaiah 40:3–5) In other words, the New Testament uses the Old Testament as much as the Old Testament uses itself.

How is he to prepare the way? One Jewish commentator says, "By purging the wicked from the land."[8] That is almost correct. As we shall see, not all the wicked are purged from the land. Some are purged in it.

---

[8] Zer Kavod, in his commentary on Malachi.

We are not told where the messenger will come. We may assume he will come to the temple, where the Lord Himself will appear. There seems to be a chronological order: first the messenger and then the Lord—not the sacred name, but the title meaning The Master (HaAdon, in Hebrew האדון). If that is the case, here we have one instance of timing that cannot be ignored: The messenger will precede the coming of the Lord. Then the Lord Himself will appear in His temple.

The temple, despised by the nations and paltry in the eyes of the returnees, will be the new residence of the Lord. It is His temple. We now know who is the Lord of whom Malachi speaks. Since the temple is described as His, and we are speaking of the temple in Jerusalem, the Lord who is to come is none other but the God of Israel. What we have, then, is a testimony to the coming of the Lord, although the prophet does not describe the manner in which He will come. Will it be a descent from heaven, an appearance at the head of an army, or the product of negotiations? All we know is that this coming is unlike like that of any human king. It may be assumed that, in speaking of the coming of the Lord, the people would think in terms of God's self-revelation at Sinai (Exodus 19:9–25; 20:18–20), of the LORD taking up residence in the tabernacle in the wilderness (Ex. 40:34–35), of the LORD coming to the temple Solomon built (2 Kings 8:10–11), or perhaps even of the revelation of God's awful glory in Ezekiel 1.

It is worth giving a few more moments of thought to the identity of the Lord (האדון). This title appears in the Hebrew Bible five more times in connection with the sacred name: The Lord, Jehovah of hosts. Each of these references appears in Isaiah (1:24; 3:1; 10:16, 33; 19:4). The title appears five more times as the Lord of all the earth (Joshua 3:11, 13; Zechariah 4:14; 6:5; Psalm 97:5), once as the Lord, Creator of the ends of the earth (Isaiah 40:28), and once in the context of denying the existence of a sovereign before whom sinners must give account (Psalm 12:5). In connection with a human king, it appears only twice (Jeremiah 22:18; 34:5).

The term therefore tends to point to the deity of the Lord. This conclusion is immediately confirmed by the way Malachi identifies the one who is to come with the LORD of Hosts, who later says I will draw near to you in judgment. Malachi's description is reminiscent of Psalm 110 where it is difficult to distinguish between one LORD and another, between God and the individual addressed by Him.

The title, LORD of Hosts, indicates God's dreadful power. He is the sovereign over the hosts of heaven and earth, ruling over angels and all heavenly bodies and all that exists on earth. Nothing can resist Him. No power can control Him. No strength is equal to His.

It is interesting to ask why He is described here as the Lord whom you seek … and the angel of the covenant whom you desire. **Where did the people learn to seek Him? Where and why did they learn to desire Him?**

Haggai and Zechariah, who prophesied a short while before Malachi, can possibly help answer that question. At the beginning of chapter two, Haggai says:

> On the twenty-first day of the seventh month, the word of the LORD came through the prophet Haggai: "Speak to Zerubbabel, son of Shealtiel, governor of Judah, to Joshua son of Jozadak, the high priest, and to the remnant of the people. Ask them, 'Who of you is left who saw this house in its former glory? How does it look to you now? Does it not seem to you like nothing?'
>
> "'But now be strong, Zerubbabel,' declares the LORD. 'Be strong, Joshua, son of Jozadak, the high priest. Be strong, all you people of the land,' declares the LORD, 'and work. For I am with you,' declares the LORD Almighty. 'This is what I covenanted with you when you came out of Egypt. And my Spirit remains among you. Do not fear.'
>
> "This is what the LORD Almighty says: 'In a little while, I will once more shake the heavens and the earth, the sea and the dry land. I will shake all nations, and what is desired by all nations will come, and I will fill this house with glory,' says the LORD Almighty. 'The silver is mine and the gold is mine,' declares the LORD Almighty. 'The glory of this present house will be greater than the glory of the former house,' says the LORD Almighty. 'And in this place I will grant peace,' declares the LORD Almighty" (vv. 1–9).

And Zechariah says:

> The word of the LORD Almighty came to me. This is what the LORD Almighty says: "I am very jealous for Zion; I am burning with jealousy for her." This is what the LORD says: "I will return to Zion and dwell in Jerusalem. Then Jerusalem will be called the Faithful City, and the mountain of the LORD Almighty will be called the Holy Mountain." This is what the LORD Almighty says: "Once again men and women of ripe old age will sit in the streets

of Jerusalem, each of them with cane in hand because of their age. The city streets will be filled with boys and girls playing there."

This is what the LORD Almighty says: "It may seem marvelous to the remnant of this people at that time, but will it seem marvelous to Me?" declares the LORD Almighty.

This is what the LORD Almighty says: "I will save My people from the countries of the east and the west. I will bring them back to live in Jerusalem; they will be My people, and I will be faithful and righteous to them as their God." This is what the LORD Almighty says: "Now hear these words, 'Let your hands be strong, so that the temple may be built.'

"This is also what the prophets said who were present when the foundation was laid for the house of the LORD Almighty. Before that time there were no wages for people or hire for animals. No one could go about their business safely because of their enemies, since I had turned everyone against their neighbor.

"But now I will not deal with the remnant of this people as I did in the past," declares the LORD Almighty. "The seed will grow well, the vine will yield its fruit, the ground will produce its crops, and the heavens will drop their dew. I will give all these things as an inheritance to the remnant of this people.

"Just as you, Judah and Israel, have been a curse among the nations, so I will save you, and you will be a blessing. Do not be afraid, but let your hands be strong." This is what the LORD Almighty says: "Just as I had determined to bring disaster on you and showed no pity when your ancestors angered Me," says the LORD Almighty, "so now I have determined to do good again to Jerusalem and Judah. Do not be afraid" (Zechariah 8:1–15).

This is not the place to discuss the history of Israel's messianic hope. Suffice it for us to recall God's promise to Adam and Eve as they were being sent out of the Garden of Eden following the first of all sins (Genesis 3:14–15). That promise is the source of the hope that beats in the breasts of the people of Israel and of the longing that has characterized the human race ever since the gates of the garden slammed shut behind our first parents. Israel learned to hope for a divine intervention from the very beginning of its national history, in the distant past and in former years.

This is the hope that was cultivated in but ever so slightly different terms through Moses (Deuteronomy 31:16, 21, 29; 32:5, 20, 29). We ought especially to note what is said in Deuteronomy 30:1–7:

> When all these blessings and curses I have set before you come on you and you take them to heart wherever the LORD your God disperses you among the nations, and when you and your children return to the LORD your God and obey Him with all your heart and with all your soul according to everything I command you today, then the LORD your God will restore your fortunes and have compassion on you and gather you again from all the nations where He scattered you.
>
> Even if you have been banished to the most distant land under the heavens, from there the LORD your God will gather you and bring you back. He will bring you to the land that belonged to your ancestors, and you will take possession of it. He will make you more prosperous and numerous than your ancestors. The LORD your God will circumcise your hearts and the hearts of your descendants, so that you may love Him with all your heart and with all your soul, and live. The LORD your God will put all these curses on your enemies who hate and persecute you.

The prophets of Israel gave expression to this hope in various ways but always in terms of a future spiritual and moral transformation of the people and the restoration and stabilization of the people's relationship with God. The reference to Moses in Malachi 4:4 is important in this context because Malachi never lost sight of the Law, even when he spoke of Israel's spiritual restoration. He saw no conflict between Law and spirituality, between loving spirituality and obedience. He believed that if we love the Lord, we will keep His commandments, and that we would not consider them onerous. The hope for which the people of Malachi's day longed had to do with the Law. The transformation of the people in the form of the Law's requirements was the expected result of the coming of the LORD to His temple.

The LORD is further described as the angel of the covenant whom you desire. The angel of the covenant is the angel appointed over the covenant God made with Israel. He is none other but the LORD Himself, the protector of the covenant. Earlier He was presented as the guardian of the marriage covenant. Now, again, the appearance of the LORD in His temple is the appearance of the angel of the covenant. What He will do is the product of His character, and His character is that of covenant guardian. If Israel will not keep covenant, the LORD of Hosts will do so by bringing on the people the punishments dictated by it.

"Behold He comes," says the LORD of Hosts. "And who can cope with the Day of His Coming? And who shall be able to stand when He is revealed? It is the LORD speaking, and He identifies Himself by the name of His glory, preparing the people for what He is about to say. The LORD of Hosts will come to His temple from which He was absent in the days of Malachi because of the sins of the priests and of the people—at the dedication of the temple in Malachi's day there was no glorious coming, as had taken place when the tabernacle was inaugurated; there was no glorious descent, as there was when Solomon's temple was dedicated. Now He will come as the angel of the covenant that the people broke, as Malachi has said, to work the work of the covenant in their hearts and to make the people anew.

You are seeking a frightening thing by desiring Him. You want Him to intervene in your history. But your expectations are misguided. You expect material and political blessings, but you ignore the most important blessing of all: being purged from sin, experiencing the joy that accompanies the kind of spiritual and moral transformation God intends to bring. God's intervention in history will be unlike anything you imagine. Who can cope with the Day of His Coming? And who shall be able to stand when He is revealed? When He appears, angels and men will fall on their faces before Him. The day of His appearance is a dreadful, shattering event. His appearance as the angel of the covenant will make it to be that kind of a day.

Malachi's warning brings to mind that of Amos: Woe to you who long for the Day of the LORD! Why do you long for the Day of the LORD? That Day will be darkness, not light. It will be as though a man fled from a lion only to meet a bear, as though he entered his house and rested his hand on the wall only to have a snake bite him. Will not the Day of the LORD be darkness, not light—pitch-dark, without a ray of brightness? (5:18–20).

Malachi's emphasis is on God's judgment in the day that He comes, which is why it is called the great and dreadful Day of the LORD (4:5). In preparation for that day, Israel must repent and mend its ways (vv. 5, 8–10), renew its covenantal undertakings (4:4), and prepare for the fulfillment of the prophet's words (4:5–6).

The phrase, the great and dreadful Day of the Lord, is taken from Joel 2:11, 31. Malachi probably borrowed the phrase, but he and Joel do not necessarily speak of the same judgment. We must not assume that identity in phrases indicates an identity of events, although that could also be the case. Such an identity can only be determined by other factors. The book of Revelation, for example, borrows phrases from all over the Scriptures, but there is no evidence that the events described in Revelation are identical to those described in the Old Testament, some of which have already occurred. We've seen Malachi and Isaiah make verbal reference to the exodus, each referring to a different event still future from their perspective, in both cases in terms of an earlier event that was not to be repeated.

That day is dreadful, says Malachi, because the LORD is like a refiner's fire and like launderer's soap. God and His activity are often represented in Scripture by fire (Exodus 19:18; 24:17; Leviticus 9:24; 10:2; Numbers 9:15; 11:1; 16:35; Deuteronomy 4:12, 24). This is one of the ways in which Scripture teaches the horror of God's holiness and His awful anger against every breach of the covenant, for a fire will be kindled by my wrath, one that burns down to the realm of the dead below. It will devour the earth and its harvests and set afire the foundations of the mountains (Deuteronomy 32:22).

A refiner's fire is the fire that a metalsmith lights to purge gold or silver from dross. In just a moment, Malachi will describe the smith's work. A launderer's soap is the cleansing material used to whiten clothing (see Jeremiah 2:22). The judgment to come does not have the destruction of the people in mind, but their purification. God purifies and sanctifies those whom He loves, treating them as a father treats his children. It is terrible, terrifying, because it is a fearful thing to fall into the hands of God.

The day of the LORD and the judgment of God are often connected in the Scriptures with fire (Isaiah 5:24; 10:16–17; 29:6; 30:27; 42:25; 66:15; Jeremiah 4:4; 21:21; 43:13; Ezekiel 15:7; 22:31; 36:5; Hosea 8:14; Joel 1:19; 2:5; Amos 1:4; 2:5; Micah 1:4; Nahum 1:6; and many others). Malachi bases his description on such uses. As we shall see in the next chapter, the words of Deuteronomy 4:21–23 probably have special reference to those in Malachi, which further explains the reference to fire.

Malachi now describes the actions of the God refiner: and He will sit like a refiner and a purifier of silver. In those days, metalsmiths would sit (most often squat) beside the small ovens they lit, melt restricted quantities of gold or silver, and carefully separate the precious metals from their dross. Judges also sat in judgment (Exodus 18:14; Psalm 9:4; Proverbs 20:8; Joel 3:2). This refiner is Israel's judge.

And He will purge the sons of Levi, and He will purge them like gold and like silver [are purged of their dross]. As we have seen, the sons of Levi are the priests, the spiritual leadership of the people, taken from the family of Aaron and the tribe of Levi (Deuteronomy 17:9; 21:5; Joshua 3:3). They too needed to be purged because they had been defiled by transgressing the Law, by their aberrant attitude to the worship of God and by their pursuit of pleasure. They were largely to blame for the people's departure from the ways of the LORD (Malachi 2:8–9, 17; 3:5).

The priests will not purge themselves. God is the one who will refine and purge them. No action is attributed to the priests; their sanctification is God's work, the result of which they will become those who bring offerings to the LORD in righteousness. God will change them. He who sees all things as they truly are will transform the unfaithful priests into those who bring offerings to the LORD in righteousness. And the offering of Judah and of Jerusalem will be pleasing to the LORD as in the distant past and in former years.

The coming of the Lord and His action in the sons of Levi are not described as the fruit or reward of Israel's action or of those of the priests. The two are sure to happen precisely because they have no connection with what Israel deserves. That is why the people should prepare for His coming by repentance. This is the only appropriate response to God's gracious intentions.

Malachi speaks of God's future actions in terms that were familiar to him and to his hearers. Ezekiel employed similar terms to describe the future, with an important difference. He described the temple and the land in terms that intimated their symbolic nature: they were impossible. The measurements given for the temple are largely without height. The measurements, seemingly so meticulous, are contradictory. Ezekiel speaks of the land as if it were oblong, far exceeding the boundaries of Israel regardless of its topography. The terms he employs are obviously symbolic, depicting the future in familiar terms but far exceeding them, much as John describes heaven in Revelation 20–22 with giant pearls and transparent gold. We learn, then, that words are not always to be taken literally; it is their meaning that must be heeded, believed, and obeyed.

Malachi promises a purification of the priests so that their offerings will be brought in righteousness. In that sense, their offerings will differ from those the priests presented in the temple in Malachi's day half-heartedly and with hands defiled by sin. Like the other prophets, Malachi insists that ritual void of morality is a hypocritical abomination, inherently unacceptable to God. The prophets of Israel did not view Jehovah as a heavenly being dependent upon the provisions brought by His worshippers. Malachi did not consider the offerings and the ritual to be means by which to obtain anything from God. He did not believe in the power of formulas, rituals, ceremonies, and the like. The worship of God was a duty men owed to God, not a means of extortion. Worship was to be an expression of gratitude and a recognition of man's dependence upon God, not a way to control Him.

All too many think of religion as a means by which man manipulates the gods: If a person or a society does something, repeats a formula, brings a sacrifice, or maintains certain standards, the gods are obliged to meet human expectations and give rain, victory in war, prosperity, a spouse, or whatever else may be sought. That is not biblical religion. Biblical religion speaks of a unilateral obligation—that of man to God—and of unilateral grace from God to man. It teaches that man has duties to God and that he never fulfills those duties. God, on the other hand, has no duties. He is free in a way that only God can be free. Any benefits man receives from God are a gift of divine grace. In other words, worship is an attribution of worth-ship to God, not a form of magic.

The priests were in the habit of bringing worthless offerings (1:6–2:9, 13) because they did not think of worship as they should. Malachi promises that, after God works to purge them, the offering of Judah and of Jerusalem will be pleasing to the LORD as in the distant past and in former years.

This will be so, Malachi says, because they will be brought in righteousness. Righteousness is an important aspect of the worship of God. A society that is not righteous has no claim to godliness. A society in which divorce is rife, where men put away their wives for pleasure, and where the family is not a sacred institute is an unrighteous society.

It is possible that the righteousness of which Malachi speaks is accommodation to the stipulations of the Law with regard to ritual. But such accommodation does not rule out the need for clean hands and social righteousness. We must take care not to vacate the message of practical reality. Those who fear God are called to social involvement, not to separatism. There is a tremendous difference between separating from sin and separating from society. Those who fear God should be deeply involved in society, as salt and light, as we shall see from what Malachi next has to say.

Return to Me and I Will Return to You

God now speaks plainly, without symbols: I will draw near ... says the LORD of Hosts. If there was any room for doubt up till now who it is that would come, He leaves no room for further doubt. He Himself will come. I will draw near to you in judgment, and I will be a witness. God will come to demand what is His.

The priests and people did not abide by the terms of the covenant. They allowed and participated in an immoral, selfish, inconsiderate society. They permitted worship that was likewise immoral, selfish, and inconsiderate of God. The LORD will now press charges and He, the Judge, will also testify against them. I will be a witness quick to testify. His testimony will be void of hesitation, with ready, unequivocal answers. He enumerates the sins that had become rampant among the priests: "I will ... testify against the magicians (Exodus 22:17; Deuteronomy 18:2, 10, 14) and the adulterers (Exodus 20:14) and those who swear falsehoods (Leviticus 19:12, see also 5:24) and who suppress the wages of hired workers (Leviticus 19:13; Deuteronomy 24:14), the widow and the orphan and the stranger they turn away [from justice] (Deuteronomy 10:18; 27:19; Jeremiah 7:6; 22:3), and do not fear me" (Deuteronomy 4:10; 6:2; 10:12, 20; 31:12; Jeremiah 32:29), says the LORD of Hosts.

Each of these sins is an indication of the erosion of national fealty, a dilution of national cohesion due to individual selfishness. They are described in a logical order. First is sin against God (magic). Then, sin against the family (adultery). Finally follow the public sins (false oaths and the oppression of the weak). Social sins have spiritual roots. Malachi, like all the prophets of Israel, believed that sins in relation to ritual lead to sins in daily life. Sins with regard to ritual are the product of a distorted view of God, which inexorably lead to a distortion of His ways and to a denial of His demands. Holiness is not a good feeling. Neither is it a sense of spiritual superiority over others. Holiness is, among other things, morality motivated by the love and fear of God.

The first sin was magic. Although idolatry was uprooted by the Babylonian exile, an idolatrous worldview remained and seems to have been strengthened. This was particularly evidenced in a tendency toward magic, which is widespread in Judaism to this very day, particularly in

Hassidic Judaism. Magic is the art of motivating spiritual powers to act according to the wishes of the magician, who uses secret formulas and codes, rituals, amulets, prayers, and sacrifices.

The second sin was selfish lust, which led to the breakdown of family life and threatened national cohesion. People had weakened family loyalties and eroded national aspirations. They were motivated above all by personal desires (in this context, "personal" is synonymous with "selfish"). Their sense of moral obligation was overridden by aroused desires that demanded satisfaction at any cost.

The third sin was swearing to falsehoods. One can safely assume that such oaths were taken in the name of the LORD in the context of the give-and-take in which humans normally engage, particularly (but not exclusively) in connection with commerce, as implied by the next sin mentioned.

The fourth sin was oppression of the poor by withholding their fairly earned wages. Men who are unfaithful to their wives cannot be expected to be faithful to their other—much lesser—undertakings, so people would hire themselves out for work, perform the work, and then have their wages withheld. Low or unpaid wages and withheld social benefits, such as sick pay, vacation, and medical insurance, are included in this sin. We are guilty if we engage in such activity toward those we employ. We are also guilty if we charge unreasonable prices or provide less quality or quantity than we have undertaken to provide in exchange for a salary.

The fifth sin was oppressing the weak members of society—the widows, orphans, and strangers. A wicked, selfish society is indifferent to single-parent families, immigrants, and illegal workers. It does not provide orphans with a fair start in life nor protect the elderly from prowling marketers who have no moral compunction. Individuals who do not endeavor to motivate their societies toward social responsibility are also guilty. This is not socialism. This is what it means to love one's neighbor. It is what the Bible describes as every person's duty toward his fellow.

God is committed to care for the weak. He is a father to the fatherless, a defender of widows (Psalm 68:5). But the priests did not imitate God. They took advantage of the weak and ruled in court in favor of those who could benefit them. Truth and justice inevitably suffered.

Malachi next describes the root of these evils: "They do not fear Me," says the LORD of Hosts. How dare Malachi level such a charge at God's people, not to speak of the priests? Since when can he read people's hearts? Let us remember that it is the LORD Himself who is addressing the people through Malachi, and God is a true reader of hearts. What is more, the people's conduct clearly disclosed the content of their hearts. Social sins run contrary to the fear of God, which can only exist where social justice as well as ritual faithfulness can be found. The fear of God teaches us that He secures justice for orphans and widows, and loves the stranger, to provide him with food and clothing (Deuteronomy 10:10; see also 27: 19; Jeremiah 7:6).

In spite of this disturbing description of the priests' sins, Malachi insists that the future of the people is as secure as is the coming of the Lord: Because I am the Lord, I do not change. It is the nature of God always to be Himself. It is His nature not to change (See Lamentations 4:1). After all, is that not what it means to be eternal? Is that not what it means to be God? Nothing can be added to Him nor subtracted from Him. He is, was, and ever shall be perfect, holy, happy, at peace with Himself, wise, gracious, righteous, never in need, never incapable of doing all His holy will.

Many read this text as if it says, because I, the Lord, do not change, you ... That is admittedly one valid way to read the Hebrew. A valid case can also be made for the reading proposed above. Because God is the Lord, He is not subject to change. He is and always will be the guardian of the covenant, in covenant with Israel and therefore faithful to the nation. Because He is what He is, you, sons of Jacob, are not destroyed. In context, the first reading seems to be the correct one.

The designation sons of Jacob is hardly a compliment. After all, Jacob is not best known for his integrity. He was unfaithful to everyone around him. It is possible that Malachi intended to remind his audience of Jacob's poor reputation as a way of reminding them who they were. In verse 8 onward, Malachi describes Israel's sins with words conjugated from the root which forms Jacob's name. The people were no better than their father and, like him, will be the objects of surprising grace.

Malachi also uses a term borrowed from the Law and used repeatedly to describe what would happen to the people if they were not faithful (Deuteronomy 28:24, 45–46, 48, 63; 29:19). They therefore had every reason to expect to be destroyed, and there was every reason to destroy them. Still, You are not destroyed. Why? Because I do not change. You are not destroyed although you deserve to be. You are not destroyed although you have broken covenant and are fully liable to the punishments that the covenant prescribes. You are not destroyed for a reason that has nothing to do with you. It is all because of Me, because of who I am, unchangeably.

Malachi's reference to the Law (his mention of Jacob and intimations of the punishments prescribed by the Law) brought to the prophet's mind other past events. From the days of your forefathers you have departed from My ways and not kept [them]. So it was at the foot of Mount Horeb, when Moses tarried on the mountain and Aaron yielded to the people's demand by creating the golden calf. So it was, time and time again, in the desert, as the people made their way to the land of promise. So it has been many times since. With equal persistence, God proved His patience and kindness. There is nothing more surprising about God than these two qualities. Think about it: Why should God be kind to rebellious humans? Why should He be patient with them in light of their stubborn waywardness?

The priests ought not to mistake such kindness for weakness or use it as an opportunity to sin. God's kindness is meant to bring them to repentance. If they will not repent, they will have to answer for their refusal.

In many instances, the priests played a major role in the people's departure from God's ways. Malachi attributes to them a long list of events in which they were notably unfaithful. Still, he says in God's name, Turn to Me, and I will turn to you. Turn from your evil, compromising ways.

Turn from them to Me. This is an intensely personal affair. Turn from your selfishness, your arrogance, your pleasure-seeking, from the enticements of the world around you, to Me. I am worth more than anything a universe of pleasures can give. God, in His kindness and grace, invites them. They are still wanted, still welcome. But they must come. They must make the conscious choice.

If they do not turn to Him, they have no grounds on which to expect Him to turn to them, except in judgment. Nor will they have grounds for complaint. They will bear the guilt of their actions. Instead of leading the people in God's ways, they followed the poor example of their fathers and have turned from God to satisfy their desires. "Turn to Me, and I will turn to you," says the LORD of Hosts. That is all they need to do.

That is all they can do. They cannot erase what they have done nor eliminate the consequences. If they but turn, the LORD of Hosts will forgive them all their trespasses and grant them His blessing.

And you said, "In what shall we return?" The priests act as if they had done nothing wrong. Perhaps they thought in such terms because their consciences had been rendered insensitive by the deceitfulness of their sins. They could identify no area in which they should turn. "What fault is there in our actions? In what area of our priestly activity or our private lives should we turn? We have taken steps to ensure that sacrifices are brought to the Lord, even if there was some slight deviation from the letter of the Law. Our divorces meet Moses's stipulations. What more can you expect?" In what shall we return?

The fact that the priests address the prophet with such a question is indication of their state. A truly spiritual person, one committed to high moral standards, would never need to ask, in what shall we return? He would know full well that there is a great deal wrong with his life, that there is a great deal that he must correct. On the other hand, someone that does not have God in his thoughts has no idea of the holiness of God. God is so far from his mind that he considers himself to be a reasonably righteous person, quite apart from whatever reality might indicate.

God, in His grace, responds by taking a simple example that will show the heinousness of the priests' actions. Will a man rob God? But you have robbed Me. And you say, 'In what have we robbed You?' In the tithe and in the goodwill offering. The Hebrew word translated robbed shares the same root as does the name Jacob. It is explained in Genesis 27:36. The term means to deceive, to obtain something by deception, to deceive someone out of what legally belongs to him. It is a kind of theft. Malachi asks in the name of the Lord, "Is it imaginable that a man would deceive God out of what belongs to Him?" This idea is so heinous, so morally unreasonable, so implausible in light of the terrible power of God, that the implied answer is obviously negative. It is imaginable that man could do such a thing. But, Malachi continues, that is exactly what you have done. Yet you have the gall to ask, "In what area of our priestly function have we robbed You?"

Malachi has moved from the general, abstract idea (Will a man rob God?) to the personal and the particular (You have robbed Me). Do you think that I am not aware of your doings? You have robbed Me in the tithes and the offerings that the people bring. It should be a full tithe taken from the best of the flocks and the herds, the fields and the orchards.

Nehemiah dealt with this same matter in the course of his second visit to Jerusalem:

> I also learned that the portions assigned to the Levites had not been given to them, and that all the Levites and musicians responsible for the service had gone back to their own fields. So I rebuked

the officials and asked them, "Why is the house of God neglected?" Then I called them together and stationed them at their posts.

All Judah brought the tithes of grain, new wine, and olive oil into the storerooms. I put Shelemiah the priest, Zadok the scribe, and a Levite named Pedaiah in charge of the storerooms and made Hanan, son of Zakkur, the son of Mattaniah, their assistant, because they were considered trustworthy. They were made responsible for distributing the supplies to their fellow Levites (**Nehemiah 13:10–13**).

If we are right in dating Malachi's prophecies a short while after Nehemiah's second visit, it is obvious that Nehemiah's actions did not affect the priests' and the people's behavior in a fundamental way. The priests continued to allow the people to bring the poorest of their flocks and their herds (Malachi 1:7–8). Apparently, they also did not require the fully prescribed amount. It is possible that some of the priests received the full tithe, but passed on to the temple only a portion. Because of such behavior, Malachi says, you are cursed with a curse, exactly as the Law stipulates (Deuteronomy 27–28).

What would you expect? It is Me that the whole nation is robbing. You think you are profited by withholding part of the tithe. In fact, you are the losers, you and the people. Bring all of the tithe to the storehouse, all of it, not just a part. We learn from these words what we surmised earlier, namely that the temple did not receive the entire tithe. It may be that the people were allowed more leeway than the Law permitted, or that the priests siphoned off a percentage for themselves.

Here is further testimony to the fact that God is not willing to accept merely part of what is coming to Him. He demands our all: all our hearts, all our souls, and all our abilities. He demands one whole day in seven and at least a tenth of our income. The measure of our generosity with whatever resources we have is often a clear indication of our heart's hidden desires and of the measure of our love for God. If you bring all that you ought, there will be food in My house. There will be all that is needed for the temple ritual.

It is worth noting that the temple, earlier described as the temple of the angel of the covenant, is here described as the house of the LORD of Hosts. Here is another hint to the identity of the divine messenger who is to come.

The prophet now faces the priests with a challenge. If they will but be faithful and generous, they will find God to be all the more faithful and all the more generous: "Try Me in this," says the LORD of Hosts, "if I will not open the floodgates of heaven and pour out on you a blessing that has no end." In spite of the prohibition to test the LORD (Exodus 17:2; Deuteronomy 6:16), God graciously condescends to be put to the test. Such humility is surprising. It also captivates the heart—except for the heart of perversely stubborn sinners.

If I will not open the floodgates of heaven. The phrase is taken from the story of the flood—a good example of what we said earlier, that similarity of wording does not necessarily imply similarity of meaning: And after the seven days, the floodwaters came on the earth. In the six hundredth year of Noah's life, on the seventeenth day of the second month— on that day all the springs of the great deep burst forth, and the floodgates of the heavens were opened. And rain fell on the earth forty days and forty nights … The waters rose and increased greatly on the earth, and the ark floated on the surface of the water. They rose greatly on the earth, and all the high mountains under the entire heavens were covered (Genesis 7:10– 12, 18–19). God will bring a flood of blessings, as He said, if I will not open the floodgates of heaven and pour out on you a blessing that has no end.

He will set aside the curse that has come upon the people due to their breach of the covenant (Deuteronomy 28:23–24). I will rebuke the devourer, and all the nations will consider you happy, because you will be a desirable land, says the LORD of Hosts.

The devourer is a swarm of locusts that apparently invaded the land. Worms and the enemy are further forces that will come upon the land and eat its fruit, as the covenant said (Deuteronomy 28:33–39, 51). "And he will not destroy the fruit of your land and the vine will not be fruitless in the field" (see Deuteronomy 28:53–57), says the LORD of Hosts. "And all the nations will consider you happy." The nations, who were witnesses to the curse that came upon you (Deuteronomy 28:37; 1 Kings 9:7; Zephaniah 2:15) will now recognize you to be blessed "because you will be a desirable land," says the LORD of Hosts.

Malachi contrasts the bitter disappointment that the priests and the people experienced with a stupendous promise. God does indeed work within the context of human history, but He is not subject to that history. He can change its direction in the teeth of all indications.

Malachi describes the blessing that Israel is to enjoy in terms reminiscent of God's promise to Israel: All peoples on earth will be blessed through you (Genesis 12:3). Through the hope that is to sustain Israel in its time of despair glistens a still greater hope, one that has to do with the goal of history: all nations, the end of times.

The Fate of the Arrogant and of Those Who Fear the Lord

Contrasting that blessed hope with the attitude of the returnees, Malachi addresses the priests in God's name: "Your words against Me are strong," says the Lord. Many interpreters take this statement as referring to what the priests actually said. So, for example, the NIV translates the statement, "You have spoken arrogantly against Me," says the LORD. But Malachi is describing God's reaction to the nature of what the priests said, not to the content or the fact of the priests' statement. It is as if He were saying, "You are acting with arrogance toward Me."

However we read the text, it is clear that God heard what the priests were saying and was displeased. And you said, 'What have we said about You?' You said, 'It is to no purpose to serve the Lord' and 'what profit [is there in that] we have remained true to Him and conducted ourselves as mourners before the LORD of Hosts?' Remained true to Him is, literally, been true to the order of His worship. The terminology is taken from the Law's description of the priests' role (For example, in Numbers 1:53, The Levites are to be responsible for the care of the tabernacle; 3:7, to perform duties for Him; 3:8, to take care of all the furnishings; 3:28, for the care of the sanctuary; 31:30, responsible for the care of the LORD's tabernacle; Deuteronomy 11:1, keep His requirements; and many other places).

Needless to say, that is the opposite of what the priests had, in fact, done. It also discloses the real motive behind the worship in which they engaged. It was not the product of a love for the LORD but an attempt to buy their way into His favor.

So far as the priests were concerned, worship was no longer a purpose in and of itself. It was viewed as a means to an end, in this case a means that did not achieve its desired end. It is to no purpose to serve the Lord, and what profit [is there in that] we have remained true to Him? What profit—what did we gain by our worship? Once relations with God become mercenary, they lose their ability to move the heart: "If I do not get what I want in exchange for my obedience, why on earth should I be obedient?" These are terrible words. Hopefully, they are unfamiliar. Do we come to worship, expecting to gain something as a reward for our worship, to "leave with something"? Or do we worship because God is worthy of worship? Do we worship out of gratitude or a mercenary at-titude?

The priests were disappointed with the poor results they had achieved in returning to Zion, restoring the temple, and renewing Jehovah's wor-ship. They tired of the moral and social cost they had to pay to be true to Him (we have remained true to Him). As far as they were concerned, those who do not give themselves over to the pleasures of life are living as mourners. They saw no profit in such a life. So they changed direction, setting aside the values that previously informed them: Now we consider the arrogant to be happy, and evil-doers prosper: they put God to the test and escaped.

Some, void of the fear of God, sinned with a high hand. They got away with it. Indeed, they profited. Seeing this, the priests were inclined to follow their example. They lost confidence in the truth of the promise, Be sure to keep the commands of the LORD your God and the stipulations and decrees He has given you. Do what is right and good in the LORD's sight and it will go well with you and you may go in and take over the good land the LORD promised on oath to your ancestors (Deuteronomy 6:17–18). They saw no reason to exert themselves in the service of the Lord. If they could not profit from such exertions, they knew where profit could be found.

In our days, there are those who view loyalty to God and a strict ob-servance of moral standards a mournful way of life. We often hear care-ful Christians, whose conscience is sensitive and who long to fear God more, being told, "Don't be so dour!" People have lost sight of the joy that comes from a cleansed conscience and of the pleasure that is the product of God's embrace. They think that nothing but the world, with its fading plastic toys and glittering trinkets, can give pleasure. They be-lieve that only a departure from God's ways and compromises with the Creator's commandments can make a man happy.

The tempter said as much in the Garden of Eden: 'You will not cer-tainly die,' the serpent said to the woman. 'For God knows that when you eat from it your eyes will be opened, and you will be like God, knowing good and evil.' When the woman saw that the fruit of the tree was good for food and pleasing to the eye, and also desirable for gaining wisdom, she took some and ate it. She also gave some to her husband, who was with her, and he ate it (Genesis 3:4–6).

Sinners have no concept of the pure, unadulterated joy spoken of in Psalm 4:8: You have filled my heart with joy more than when their grain and new wine abound.[9]

Then, in contrast with the sinful and worldly, those who feared the LORD spoke one to another. In response to the words of the arrogant, some chose to strengthen each other with words of encouragement. Malachi does not tell us what they said, but it is not difficult to imagine that they reminded one another of the holiness of God, His grace, His greatness, and the righteousness of His commandments, of the reward of the faithful, and the punishment of the wicked. The practice adopted by those who feared the LORD reminds us of the value of church life and of Christian friendship.

Those who feared the LORD spoke one to another. They strengthened each other in the ways of the Lord. They encouraged each other in the face of difficulties and strengthened their hands in the face of the circumstances. We need each other. We need the company of others who fear God, who are spiritual, loving, and courageous, and who can strengthen our hands in our moments of weakness, such as every individual experiences. God accords such fellowship His full attention: the LORD listened and heard. He listened no more than He listened to the words of those who did not fear Him, but His response to what He heard was different.

And [He] wrote a book of remembrance [to be kept] before Him about those who feared the LORD and thought on His name. The imagery is familiar to all who are acquainted with the practices of kings in the ancient Near East. Artaxerxes had such a book (the book of the Chronicles, the record of his reign, Esther 6:1). Those who thought on His name are those who attribute worship to God and therefore value His name, remain faithful, come what may, and worship God sacrificially.

"And they will be Mine," says the LORD of Hosts. They will be Mine in a special way. They will be My beloved, My cherished ones on the Day which I am making. God is referring to the day of judgment, described at the beginning of this chapter. God is presently "making" that day. He is engaged in its preparation. At that time, when the Lord will come to His

---

[9] David Brainard, early American missionary to the Indians, quoted those words as he lay on his deathbed, coughing up blood and struggling for breath. He knew a joy, pure and unshakeable, that none but those who know God ever experience.

temple and the unrighteous will be punished, He will treat the faithful, who supported each other, as a special possession.

The wicked will perish and the faithful, in contrast with the wicked, will be treasured as God's prized possession. In Exodus 19:5; Deuteronomy 14:2; 26:18, the term special possession is used to refer to the nation as a whole. Malachi is saying that the remnant of the people, the faithful among the nation, will inherit the nation's place. God's purposes for Israel will be accomplished in the faithful remnant. Once again, by quoting the Law, Malachi is reverting to the Law, which serves as the basis of his message.

And I will have mercy on them like a man has mercy on his son who serves him. The faithful love that God showed Israel when He brought them out of Egypt (Exodus 4:22) will be renewed. God will save the remnant, just as He saved Israel from Egypt so many years ago. This change in the ways God treats Israel will bring about a spiritual and moral transformation in the priests. You will again see the difference between a righteous and an evil man, between one who serves God and one who does not. They will then revert to judging the people in faithful accordance with the commandments of the Lord.

LET'S SUMMARIZE

1. The grace, goodness, and faithfulness of God are our only solid grounds of life and for hope of the future. These are solid grounds indeed. Let us build our lives on them.

2. It is God who changes people spiritually and morally. He does so to those whom He has chosen, removing sin from them and making them acceptable in His eyes. We should turn to Him so that He might turn to us and continually work that change in our hearts.

3. God is faithful to His covenants. We should be so to ours. He is the guardian of the covenant and will hold us to account. Formality without morality is hypocrisy. It vacates our ceremonies of value and is, in fact, a breach of covenant.

4. Israel learned from the Law and the prophets to hope for a Savior. We should have our aspirations tuned to our hopes and our hopes guided and motivated by the Word of God.

5. Sin makes us spiritually and morally insensitive. Let's beware of the slightest inklings of sin in our lives. Let's cultivate a careful godliness.

6. The day of judgment will surely come. We should prepare for it by living as those who believe it will come.

LET'S PRAY

Lord of Hosts,

We are quick to doubt You and to trust ourselves.

Teach us to submit to Your leadership of our lives

and to willingly submit to whatever You bring,

knowing that You work all things to Your glory

and to the good of those You have chosen to love.

Teach us to deny ourselves

and to love and serve Your Son, our Savior.

As we undergo the struggles of life,

teach us to treat one another with love and respect

and to cultivate the fellowship of believers in the church

until we come to Your eternal kingdom,

where we shall enjoy the pleasantness

of brethren together in unity.

May we love Your Son earnestly

and entrust our salvation into His sure hands

so that we follow Him rather than the temptations of the world,

that we overcome our spiritual laziness,

keep constant watch over our spirits,

and at last be granted sanctification

and the joy of honoring and enjoying You forever.

In the name of our great Savior, Jesus, Your Son.

Amen.

SUBJECTS FOR DISCUSSION AND STUDY

- What principles for understanding the Scriptures may we derive from this chapter of Malachi?

- Describe, on the basis of this chapter, human society as it should be.

- What is the role of the Law according to Malachi's use of and reference to it in this chapter?

CHAPTER 6

The Day Is Coming:
Remember Moses, My Servant
(MALACHI 4:1–6)

"For behold, the Day is coming, burning like an oven, and all the arrogant and all the evildoers will be like straw—the Day that is coming will burn them," says the LORD of hosts, who will not leave them a root or a branch. "But to you, who fear My name, a sun of righteousness and of healing will shine. And you will spread out [in the pasture] like fatted calves and you shall trample evil ones because they will be ashes under the palms of your feet in the Day that I am making," says the LORD of Hosts.

"Remember the Law of Moses My servant, which I commanded him in Horeb [to set] over all Israel laws and commands. Behold I am sending you Elias the prophet before the coming of the great and dreadful Day of the Lord, and he will turn the hearts of fathers to sons and the hearts of sons to their fathers, lest I come and strike the earth with an irreversible curse."

Differences

For behold, the Day is coming. The Day to which Malachi refers here is the day of judgment. That day is burning like an oven. The verb is in the present tense: The fire is already burning, just as the Lord is already making that day, and the day is already coming. The fire that appeared in chapter three appears again, with an important difference. That fire was to purify the sons of Levi. This fire will destroy sinners. Perhaps it is the same fire, purging some and destroying others.

God chooses to treat people differently. No one can prevent Him from doing so or complain of injustice. Does the potter not have a right to do whatever he wishes with the material he has at hand? Has he no right to make of one part of the lump a gloriously beautiful vessel and of the other a piece fit for the burning? Who deserves mercy? No human has a claim on divine mercy; it is a unilateral act of grace, given at will by the giver. Mercy is contrary to any human deserving—not the product of it—and God gives mercy to whomsoever He wills, and He gives mercy richly, generously, to an amazing extent.

But He does not give it to all as the next statement shows. And all the arrogant and all the evildoers, considered earlier by the priests to be happy in the previous chapter, will be like straw quickly burnt, incapable of withstanding the fire, "the Day that is coming will burn them," says the LORD of hosts, "who will not leave them a root or a branch." This is a picture of complete, irrevocable destruction at the hand of the LORD. Nothing shall remain of the arrogant and of all the evildoers in the soil (a root) or upon the ground (a branch). In spite of appearances, the strength of the wicked is nothing compared to God's. They are but straw. His anger is like a raging fire; it consumes straw effortlessly. Men should not boast of their strength. God is mightier than them by far!

But, in premeditated contrast with the fate of the arrogant (Malachi has drawn many contrasts in these chapters), to you among the priests, those who fear My name, a sun of righteousness and of healing will shine. Not fire but light. Not trouble and disease but healing. Not sin punished but faithful (righteous) covenant grace and forgiving sin.

And you will spread out [in the pasture] like fatted calves. Rather than being restricted as the returnees were in the tiny enclave surrounding Jerusalem, jammed between Edomites and Samaritans, they will spread out like fatted calves, the epitome of health and happiness.

And you shall trample evil ones. The symbolic action of conquest is taken from Psalm 110:1, which in turn is reminiscent of Joshua 10:23–25, where we read:

> They brought the five kings out of the cave—the kings of Jerusalem, Hebron, Jarmuth, Lachish, and Eglon. When they had brought these kings to Joshua, he summoned all the men of Israel and said to the army commanders who had come with him, "Come here and put your feet on the necks of these kings." So they came forward and placed their feet on their necks. Joshua said to them, "Do not be afraid; do not be discouraged. Be strong and courageous.

This is what the LORD will do to all the enemies you are going to fight."

None should think lightly of God's mercy. There will be those who will spread out like fatted calves, and there will be those who are trampled underfoot, burnt on that dreadful day of the LORD like straw, with neither root nor branch left behind.

There are only two classes of people: the justly lost and the graciously redeemed.

The faithful will trample the evildoers. "They will be ashes under the palms of your feet in the Day that I am making," says the LORD of Hosts. Your victory, now so unlikely in light of the evildoers' success, will be seen to be as mighty a work of God as was the conquest of the land from the five kings in Joshua's day.

That day is all of God's making and is, as we have seen, in the process of formation. The verbs are in the present continuous tense: is coming, is burning. We saw above that the day was in the making. Future realities will be the product of a divine intervention, not of natural processes. They will be the product of a divine process that God has set in motion. There is continuity within divine activity because He and His actions are in complete harmony. There is no inconsistency. On the other hand, there is a fundamental discontinuity with the sinful and sin-affected processes of this world until the restoration of all things in their original order, as it was in the beginning.

Remember

Malachi has made extensive indirect and direct references to the Law and to the prophets. He now seals his message with a call to turn from the breaches of the covenant he has described and to be faithful to God and to his Law: Remember the Law of Moses my servant, which I commanded him in Horeb [to set] over all Israel laws and commands.

To remember is not merely to recall, but to recall with a view to observance: Remember the Sabbath day. How? By keeping it holy (Exodus 20:8). God is not interested in an intellectual exercise or a fond memory. He calls for action. The priests and all who fear God are called to carry out the requirements of the Law. Moses My servant is the honorific title accorded to Moses in Exodus 14:31; Numbers 12:7; Deuteronomy 34:5. Horeb is Mount Sinai (Exodus 3:1; 33:6; Deuteronomy 1:6; 4:10; and others).

The Law's commandments are, primarily, the Ten Commandments. Malachi is apparently reflecting the wording of Deuteronomy 4:1–2: Now, Israel, hear the decrees and laws I am about to teach you. Follow them so that you may live and may go in and take possession of the land the LORD, the God of your ancestors, is giving you. Do not add to what I command you and do not subtract from it, but keep the commands of the LORD your God that I give you. It is also worth looking at Deuteronomy 5:1–4. Malachi was deeply immersed in the language of the Old Testament; as Spurgeon said of Bunyan, we can say of Malachi, "prick him and his blood flows bibline."[10]

Malachi thought of Israel's redemption in terms of the Law. He could not think of the Law as anything but rules and commands. They are to be obeyed. Malachi's view of the fear of God was inseparable from day-to-day obedience in the mundane things of life. As we saw, to love God is to obey Him. To obey Him is to honor Him. To honor Him is to give Him His due in terms of actions and intent.

To remember with the intention to obey: that was the duty of the priests and of the people. It remains the duty of all who fear God. But that is not the be-all and end-all of the spiritual life. That life begins with a transformation that God works in human hearts. God must first purify our hearts. Only then can we serve Him appropriately. But there is still more to it than that. Behold I am sending you Elias the prophet before the coming of the great and dreadful Day of the LORD.

In Malachi 3:1, God promised the people to send Elias (spelled differently in Hebrew than Elijah, but referring to the same person; see 1 Kings 1:3). This is a reiteration of that promise. He will be sent to the people (I am sending you), not against them. Elias will not come to condemn but to prepare them for the coming of the day.

This is the sole Old Testament reference to the coming of Elijah in the last days to herald the coming of Messiah. Elijah/Elias will come before the coming of the great and dreadful Day of the LORD (see Joel 2:11; 2:31). Note again the reference to the horror of that day. The coming of the LORD will be as terrible as it will be wonderful—an odor of life for some and of death for others.

What purpose will be served by Elijah's coming? He will prepare the way of the LORD (3:1). His coming will be terrible, as will be the day he

---

[10] C.H. Spurgeon, *The Full Harvest* (Edinburgh: Banner of Truth, 1973), 159.

comes to announce. But there is another contrast, for God is drawing another difference.

To the wicked, He will be terrible. Recall, that great and dreadful day of the LORD is like a refiner's fire for some among the priests and the people. Now Elijah is described as coming for the good of those whose filth is to be purged: and he will turn the hearts of fathers to sons and the hearts of sons to their fathers. One Israeli commentator[11] puts it this way: "He will draw the hearts of the fathers to the sons, as he united the hearts of the people of Israel, who had been divided into the worshippers of God and the worshippers of Baal in the days of Ahab, and they were untied all with the one conscious truth that 'The Lord, he is God' "(1 Kings 18:39).

The meaning of this verse was the subject of intense discussion by the rabbis.[12] The majority concluded that Malachi was referring to the peace that Elijah will bring to the world because he will resolve the conflicts that exist between fathers and sons. The rabbis had nothing to say about the manner in which this wonderful feat would be accomplished nor does Malachi, and we will not add to his words.

However we understand this statement, Elijah's work is to be accomplished, lest I come and strike the earth with an irreversible curse (חרם), says the Lord. In other words, he will come to ensure that such a curse is not imposed.

The priests are challenged to remember and to observe the Law and the prophets and to teach the people accordingly. Otherwise, the land (referring to the land of Israel) will be stricken with an irreversible curse—"irreversible" because the term used here is not the one Malachi has used earlier. It is the term used to describe the utter and irreversible destruction of Jericho (Joshua 6:18–19, 26).

Malachi describes the future without the universal implications we learn from other passages of God's Word, even though he says that the LORD is worthily worshipped among the nations (1:11, 14). Malachi deals exclusively with Israel. He makes no reference to the renewal of the Davidic dynastic reign, which would include the nations, nor does he speak of the renovation of nature, the judgment of the nations, or the defeat of idolatry.

This is not to intimate that Malachi entertained no such hope. For one so thoroughly immersed in the Old Testament, it is impossible that

[11] S. L. Gordon in his commentary on Malachi.
[12] Eduyot chapter 8, seventh Mishnaya.

he should share the hope inculcated there. But he does not refer to these features in his prophecy, and we should not attribute to him anything he does not say. We must allow Malachi to say only that which God gave him to say, no more. That is part of our respect for God's Word and recognition of the mode of inspiration. Other truths must be quarried from other portions of Scripture.

Malachi presents the coming of the LORD in terms of the covenant God made with Israel at Horeb. The faithfulness to which the prophet called the nation in the worship of God and the social and familial moral conduct expected in society and in the family, including commercial enterprise, is defined in terms of the law of the covenant given to Israel through Moses at Horeb.

In light of the problems with which Malachi was sent to deal, this is understandable. The prophet had to call the people back to a sense of national destiny that would require them to maintain a national distinctiveness. A discussion of the universal implications of the future would not serve that purpose. From this we may deduce an important lesson: It is not enough to speak the truth. For our words to be like apples of gold in a silver frame, they need to be spoken in season.

We do not to have to tell the whole story, answer all the questions, and fill in all the blanks before we have fulfilled our duty. It is wise to relate our explanations to the circumstances rather than try to be exhaustive (and therefore exhausting) every time we present the Gospel. Malachi spoke of the future in terms of the pressing needs of his time. His message was designed to encourage the faithful to persist in their faithfulness and to warn the unfaithful to turn from their sins. Such turning is described in terms of familial and social integrity and of the faithful, heartfelt observance of the worship of God in the temple. But the temple ritual is thought of as purified, sincere, and therefore acceptable to the Lord. Malachi tailored his message to his times.

In Closing

The book deals with four major topics: Edom, worship, marriage, and the day of the Lord. The last three are framed in terms of the Law. There is no lack of social sensitivity (3:5, not to speak of what he has to say about marriage), such as characterized all of Israel and Judah's prophets, but that is not the prophet's main interest.

While Malachi deals with issues related to his time, his vision exceeds it. His extensive reference to the Law, especially to the book of Deuteronomy, indicates that Malachi viewed his period in light of the Law and of the promises of God in the Law: the people transgressed the Law and broke covenant. God said He would punish some according to the law of the covenant and that He will withhold punishments from others. The latter He will purge so that they come to know the difference between right and wrong and, therefore serve Him acceptably.

Malachi's emphasis on the Law naturally led him to emphasize the role of the priests, as well as to frame his thoughts of the future with reference to the Law. His closing call to remember the Law is hardly surprising in this age of selfish compromises. It is a call we all need to hear.

It is probable that Malachi also had in mind passages such as the one following as he framed his message under inspiration of the Spirit of God:

Be careful not to forget the covenant of the LORD your God that He made with you; do not make for yourselves an idol in the form of anything the LORD your God has forbidden. For the LORD your God is a consuming fire, a jealous God.

After you have had children and grandchildren and have lived in the land a long time—if you then become corrupt and make any kind of idol, doing evil in the eyes of the LORD your God and arousing His anger, I call the heavens and the earth as witnesses against you this Day that you will quickly perish from the land that you are crossing the Jordan to possess.

You will not live there long but will certainly be destroyed. The LORD will scatter you among the peoples, and only a few of you will survive among the nations to which the LORD will drive you. There you will worship man-made gods of wood and stone, which cannot see or hear or eat or smell.

But if from there you seek the LORD your God, you will find Him if you seek Him with all your heart and with all your soul. When you are in distress and all these things have happened to you, then in later days you will return to the LORD your God and obey Him. For the LORD your God is a merciful God; He will not abandon or destroy you or forget the covenant with your ancestors, which He confirmed to them by oath (Deuteronomy 4:23–31; note the reference to the latter days).

Such warnings connect easily with Malachi's message in general and with his reference to the angel of the covenant. The similarities between Malachi and passages like the one just quoted are, surely, not the product of chance. Israel was exiled to Babylon because the people sinned, exactly as the Law warned would happen. Their society was promiscuous, materialistic, idolatrous, and void of mercy.

In exile, the people sought the LORD and were returned to the land. It would have been natural for them to think that the end of times had arrived (v. 30). God had said, in later days you will return to the LORD your God and obey Him. For the LORD your God is a merciful God; He will not abandon or destroy you or forget the covenant with your ancestors, which He confirmed to them by oath. He would not forget, but would they? Hence Malachi's closing call, Remember the Law of Moses My servant, which I commanded him in Horeb.

Finally, Malachi was sent to call the people back from the despair dictated by their circumstances, away from the spiritual and moral lethargy that despair had encouraged. They were to look beyond their circumstances, to their duties and to the promises of God. We would do well to be occupied with the same in our day and to be motivated by the same confidence that drove Malachi and gave substance to his message.

LET'S SUMMARIZE

1. God makes great promises to those who fear His name. Do we fear Him? If we do, how is our fear expressed?

2. Fear of His name should drive us away from sin. Name three sins from which you now wish to abstain.

3. To fear God's name is to keep covenant with Him, to remember His Law, and to obey it.

4. Evil shall be conquered and the faithful blessed. This will be the work of God and His alone. There is no room for Christian triumphalism, or for physical or political conquest. His kingdom is not established by worldly means.

As I hope you will see, the New Testament teaches the same principles as does the Old. It is not difficult to preach the Gospel from the Old Testament without resorting to spiritualization or any of the interpretational manipulations that are so common in modern Christian pulpits. If we will but allow the Old Testament to speak for itself, it will inexorably lead to the Gospel of Jesus, the Messiah.

LET'S PRAY

Great and terrible Lord,

dreadful and righteous,

merciful and kind,

grant us to fear Your Name and

remember Your Law to do it.

Hasten the day when You will shine upon Your people

as a sun of righteousness.

Oh God of mercy,

work in our hearts

and in the hearts of the people of Israel

so that we and they observe the Law of Your Covenant

and trust in the Lord Jesus Christ.

In Jesus's saving name.

Amen.

QUESTIONS FOR DISCUSSION AND STUDY

• How does this chapter serve as a fitting summary of previous chapters?

• Describe the latter days on the basis of what is said in the book of Malachi.

- Discuss the practical implications of Malachi's message concerning marriage and divorce.

- Compare Malachi's message with the Gospel of Jesus the Messiah.

- Summarize what is said by Malachi about the Law.

CPSIA information can be obtained
at www.ICGtesting.com
Printed in the USA
LVOW12s0005290416

485865LV00001B/1/P